The Watchman's Playbook

Strategies to Win Through Prayer

Written by

C. Shaemun Webster

Chayil Publishing House

Chayil Publishing House *(Sister and Son, LLC.)* Alabama, USA

Copyright © 2022 Carey Shaemun Webster

ISBN-13: 979-8-9861818-0-6
ISBN-13: 979-8-9861818-1-3 (e-book)

***

First Printing, 2022

Dedication

I personally believe that dedications serve as a place of honor, recognition, and appreciation at summits of success. I realize that I have reached this place and have come this far because of God's favor and mandate on my life. This is the Lord's doing, and it's marvelous in my eyes (Psalm 118:23). I thank Him for enabling me to do the Work in which He sent me to do and for making all things possible.

I've always known that I would do great exploits in the earth. I always knew, even as a youngster, that my life would be of service unto the Lord and impacting lives for His glory. I **never** doubted the call, nor did my family. My family was very intentional with the cultivation of my faith, exposure to leadership development and having access to cutting-edge knowledge. As I reflect and give thanks, I dedicate my first publication to my mother, Kimberly R. Oden-Webster, and my sister, K. Miaya-Ree Webster. My father transitioned into eternity in 2015 — but I knew he left this earth with a day like this in view concerning his son; "Da-Da," (Carey L. Webster), this one is for you. I would be remiss, if I did not honor the lineage from whence I've come — whose prayers, instruction and love groomed me for such a time as this: the late Ruby P. Webster (grandmother), Roland Webster (grandfather), S. Catheline Oden (grandmother), Walter Oden (grandfather) and Rev. Eddie L. King (great-uncle).

I come from a family of faith, who believes in the power of prayer. Prayer has always been the essence of our faith. We prayed when times were well and when times were challenging. Prayer always brought us through. Hence, I understand now why the mantle and passion for intercession is on my life; now, God has allowed me to develop a resource for the earth with downloads from heaven for believers of all time to win in every season via strategies in prayer.

This book is also dedicated to my family, The Oden's, Williams', Webster's, for your unwavering support and love. Thank you for always believing in the call on my life and making sure everything I need to serve this present age, is provided. I honor you. To my all my close friends who create my 'village' — thank you for believing in me, entrusting me to be your leader and friend, I love you! I couldn't have made it without your push and prayers.

This book is dedicated to the people whom I pour my all out to and I do it with a glad heart — my church family, The Tower of

Prayer Church, and The Ark Church Huntsville! You all are my heartbeat. I LOVE my people! Assembly of Pioneers, Fresh Start Family and all partners who are a part of the streams of the anointing, I dedicate this work to you.

Finally, this book is dedicated to all future intercessors whom God will raise up to be watchmen on the wall. May God activate grace in you as you press toward the mark for the prize of the high calling of God in Christ Jesus.

Love,

C. Shaemun Webster

Table of Contents

Introduction

The Connection

Located in every human being is the wiring for spiritual connection. Sin is strong but not dominant enough to destroy our ability to connect or reconnect with God at any time – thanks to Jesus. **Hebrews 4:15-16 (NIV)** says, *"For we do not have a high priest who is unable to empathize with our weaknesses, but we have one who has been tempted in every way, just as we are—yet he did not sin. Let us then approach God's throne of grace with confidence, so that we may receive mercy and find grace to help us in our time of need."*

The Scripture declares, "the wages of sin is death, but the gift of God is eternal life," [Romans 6:23] — death is disconnection (the state of being isolated or detached, termination of the connection of one thing to another). Sin brought death into the complexities of human life and that death element also brought about disconnections. Think about it, there's emotional disconnection, when you're separated from people you care about, and there's also the disconnection that occurs when a cord is unplugged, or a source of energy or information is broken. During the Fall of Mankind in Genesis 3, when man rebelled against God, the disconnect transpired; man was estranged from close fellowship with God, communication lines were broken, and power was withdrawn.

For the sin of this one man, Adam, caused death to rule over many. But even greater is God's wonderful grace and his gift of righteousness, for all who receive it will live in triumph over sin and death through this one man, Jesus Christ. **Romans 5:17 (NLT)**

The adversary's agenda is found in John 10:10 — to steal, kill and destroy and Jesus' purpose and mission is to bring life so that we might have it more abundantly. Jesus brings mankind restoration of the original connection!

All humans are pre-wired for spiritual connection and to compliment that wiring, the True and Living God has made all believers a promise that if we communicate with Him, He'd communicate with us. Set your hope on God's promise to us in Isaiah 58:9 (GNT), *"When you pray, I will answer you. When you call to me, I will respond."* Let's take a moment, pause, and ponder on that truth — the Creator yearns, desires and has made provision for ways for all mankind to communicate with Him. God reassures us in His Word with this truth. The challenge that has presented itself for believers is how to effectively communicate with God — prayer, also known as intercession.

The Cause

I have had many to ask before, "If God is in control, sovereign and all powerful, why do we have to pray? Why are we called to pray and what good does our prayers do?". The reason why we are called to pray is two-fold: so that the finite believer might have an open line of communication at all times with the infinite God; and, we are in warfare. Satan is still waging war to keep mankind disconnected from God. The adversary does not want anyone to be in fellowship with God, be able to reach God or spend eternity with God — because he [Satan] can't.

"For though we walk (live) in the flesh, we are not carrying on our warfare according to the flesh and using mere human weapons. For the weapons of our warfare are not physical [weapons of flesh and blood], but they are mighty before God for the overthrow and destruction of strongholds," **2 Corinthians 10:3-5 (AMPC)**

Prayer is a tool, weapon, and kingdom resource for all believers. Prayer is more than a posture, but prayer is also a place. That's right, prayer is a place — it's a place where believers can retreat to release and receive! Prayer is not one-sided — where we express our sentiments to God and walk away empty-handed, uninformed, or unequipped to win the good fight of faith.

There is not one situation that is beyond God's ability to intervene. We all face situations, challenges, circumstances, difficulties, hardships that are beyond our strength to change alone. Change requires supernatural intervention. The Bible says in James 1:2 that believers face trials of many kinds. God's strategy for supernatural interventions for our situations is intercession.

Intercession is the gateway to supernatural interventions. Intercession is putting yourself in God's place; it is having His mind and His perspective while you're praying. You can't get above circumstances unless you know that you have the ear of God. Intervene means **action taken to improve a situation.** Let's help it make sense — when you intercede [pray], with God's mind and perspective [His Word], **you give God access to act and improve a situation!**

We all have situations that need supernatural intervention, and we agree that intercession is the gateway/conduit to supernatural intervention, but we don't all intercede. Why? **Time is not an excuse for the lack of a prayer life. You have a theology issue [what you believe about God].** People do not pray for one of these reasons:

You feel as if God doesn't hear *you.* Feelings of unworthiness due to sin in your life and feeling like God hears "other" people prayers before He would even consider hearing yours. When you don't feel close to the Lord, you don't pray. **Your lack of holiness doesn't impact His hearing ability.**

God is known as *El Shama* — *The God who hears "me."*

> **Jeremiah 33:3 (NKJV)** — *'Call to Me, and I will answer you, and show you great and mighty things, which you do not know.'*

> **Jeremiah 29:12 (NIV)** — *Then you will call on me and come and pray to me, and I will listen to you.*

You fear an unfulfilled request. *"God probably won't do this/that"* *This is evidence that doubt is present.*

> **1 John 5:14 (NKJV)** *"This is the confidence we have in approaching God: that if we ask anything according to his will, he hears us."*

This is because we are constantly plagued with doubts, wondering if He hears us or listens to our prayers.

You have an unhealthy perspective of your position with God. The Scripture gives us the relationship we have in prayer which gives us the position from which we should pray from — as a *child of God.*

> **Romans 8:15 (NLT)** — *So you have not received a spirit that makes you fearful slaves. Instead, you received God's Spirit when he adopted you as his own children. Now we call him, "Abba, Father."*
>
> **Matthew 6:6 (NIV)** — *But when you pray, go into your room, close the door, and pray to your Father, who is unseen. Then your Father, who sees what is done in secret, will reward you.*

The Command

Jesus says in **Luke 18:1 (NKJV)**, *"that men always ought to pray and not lose heart."* The Greek word translated for pray is — *proseuchomai which means, [make prayer, supplicate, worship, prayer to God].* Prayer is a form of worship unto God, and we are encouraged to do so in Spirit and in Truth [bringing our realities to God, not hiding anything from Him.] God has extended a righteous invitation to all believers to pray, always by bringing Him our realities; and when we do so, we worship the Father. [Also see, 1 Thessalonians 5:16-18, Psalm 116:2, Ephesians 6:18].

The Calling

"So you, son of man: I have made you a watchman for the house of Israel; therefore you shall hear a word from My mouth and warn them for Me." **Ezekiel 33:7 (NKJV)**

This book is in your hand because you are in tune with your spiritual wiring to communicate with God. You are reading this book right now because you yearn to have a successful communication line with God. The LORD is making an ancient call for *watchmen* to return to the wall and role of the *watchman* be brought to the forefront of hearts and minds of believers. Remember earlier I mentioned how prayer is more than a posture? It's a position we hold on earth and God calls us, "watchmen" according to Ezekiel 33:7.

The loss of the full understanding of this function, personally and corporately, has catapulted the world into an ever-increasing conflict between good and evil. Watchmen are God-authorized, legal guardians over the affairs of the Earth. Intercessors themselves are God-authorized guardians and guards. This book reveals and solidifies the importance of intercessors understanding the mind behind spiritual warfare, the participants, and perspectives of it in its totality.

You are called to prayer. You are called to stand in the gap. You are called to be a kingdom communicator for such a time as this. Give thanks that Jesus came to reconnect us back to the Father according to — **John 14:13 (ESV)**, *"Whatever you ask in my name, this I will do, that the Father may be glorified in the Son."*

O watchman, take your post, make your petition known and get ready to see God's power be made manifest in your life, family, ministry, industry, and the world.

O Jerusalem, I have posted watchmen on your walls; they will pray day and night, continually. Take no rest, all you who pray to the LORD. **Isaiah 62:6 (NLT)**

_____

Sign Your Name Above

To commit to being one of the Lord's Watchmen

What is a Watchman?

"So you, son of man: I have made you a watchman for the house of Israel; therefore you shall hear a word from My moth and warn them for Me." **Ezekiel 33:7 (NKJV)**

God is making an ancient call and role of the watchman and bringing into the forefront of hearts and minds of Christians seeking the Lord in these days of accelerating adversity. The loss of the full understanding of this function, personally and corporately, has catapulted the world into an ever-increasing conflict between good and evil.

Watchmen are God-authorized, legal guardians over the affairs of the Earth. The word "watchmen" is translated from the Hebrew word Shamar or Shomer and the Hebrew Word — 'tsaphah.' It appears 468 times in the Scripture and is translated "watchman" eight times. Other alternate translations are keep, guard, guardian, keeper, watch, observe, heed, or preserve. A watchman can be defined in several ways.

Shamar — to guard, to keep, have charge of, guard, observe, give heed, keep watch and guard, protect, save life, to watch and observe

Shomer — Jewish legal guardian entrusted with the custody and care of another's object.

God has granted and entrusted watchmen with legal guardianship with the custody and care of everything that belongs to Him in the earth realm. Man was authorized authority.

Genesis 1:28 (AMP) — *And God blessed them [granting them certain authority] and said to them, "Be fruitful, multiply, and fill the earth, and subjugate it [putting it under your power]; and rule over (dominate) the fish of the sea, the birds of the air, and every living thing that moves upon the earth."*

Genesis 2:15 (KJV) — *"And the Lord God took the man and put him into the garden of Eden to dress it and to keep it."*

Keeping with this theme, it translates into Hebrew, Shamar (H8104), same term used for watchman, to watch over, protect, preserve. Hence, Adam was the first authorized watchman in scripture. Man's only duty, assignment, and call was to watch over the place, the territory that God had given Him. The reason why the world is in the condition and shape it is in now is because the authorized watchman left his post allowing sin to creep in. We are not left without help, though. As noted in the following scriptures, God is the model watchman.

Psalm 121:2-4 (KJV) — My help cometh from the Lord, which made heaven and earth. 3 He will not suffer thy foot to be moved: he that **keepeth** thee will not slumber. 4 Behold, he that **keepeth** Israel shall neither slumber nor sleep.

Psalm 121: 5-8 (NIV) — The Lord **watches** over you— the Lord is your shade at your right hand; 6 the sun will not harm you by day, nor the moon by night. 7 The Lord will keep you from all harm— he will watch over your life; 8 the Lord will watch over your coming and going both now and forevermore.

Jeremiah 1:12 (NIV) — The Lord said to me, "You have seen correctly, for I am **watching** to see that my word is fulfilled."

As you return to your post, pray this prayer with me.

Prayer

Father, You are the Originator, Creator and Maker of all things good and true. In your insurmountable wisdom, Your Word declares in Ezekiel 33:7 that you have created me to be a watchman; to guard, keep watch, to protect and save life through strategic intercession. I receive by faith the fortitude to pray without ceasing, to watch over all areas I am assigned to cover in prayer. I thank You, Lord that as I watch and pray, I clearly hear the Word of the Lord for such a time as this. My life will never be void of Your Word or instructions for each season and stage of my life. It is so, in Jesus' name, Amen.

Reflect and write what the Lord is sharing with you during your time of prayer.

_____

_____

_____

_____

_____

_____

_____

_____

_____

_____

_____

_____

_____

_____

_____

_____

_____

_____

_____

_____

_____

_____

_____

NOTES

The Calling of a Watchman

6 I have set watchmen upon thy walls, O Jerusalem, which shall never hold their peace day nor night: ye that make mention of the Lord, keep not silence, 7 And give him no rest, till he establishes, and till he makes Jerusalem a praise in the earth.

8 The Lord hath sworn by his right hand, and by the arm of his strength, Surely I will no more give thy corn to be meat for thine enemies; and the sons of the stranger shall not drink thy wine, for the which thou hast laboured:

Isaiah 62:6-8 (KJV)

In Isaiah 62:6–7, the prophet speaks about praying for Jerusalem with the same careful attention as a watchman on the walls of a city. The watchman holds the security of the people in his hands. God is calling on us to be like those watchmen. We must be constantly alert to the dangers which surround Israel (the people of God). We must call out to God to keep (shomer) His promises.

The job of a watchman was so critical to the safety and provision of the people, readers of this passage in biblical times would have clearly understood the importance of being a watchman in the spiritual realm. We are called to partner with God in this level of oversight in the spirit. In verse eight, He promises that He will "with a strong arm" keep the crops safe from enemies, another clear allusion to "watchman," which identifies Him as the Watchman of Israel.

Luke 18:1 (AMP) — *"Now Jesus was telling the disciples a parable to make the point that at all times they ought to pray and not give up and lose heart"*

Matthew 26:41 (NLT) — *"Keep watch and pray, so that you will not give in to temptation. For the spirit is willing, but the body is weak!"*

Matthew 26:41 (GW) — *"Stay awake, and pray that you won't be tempted. You want to do what's right, but you're weak."*

Matthew 26:39-46 (NIV) — *39 Going a little farther, he fell with his face to the ground and prayed, "My Father, if it is possible, may this cup be taken from me. Yet not as I will, but as you will." 40 Then he returned to his disciples and found them sleeping. "Couldn't you men keep watch with me for one hour?" he asked Peter. 41 "Watch and pray so that you will not fall into temptation. The spirit is willing, but the flesh is weak." 42 He went away a second time and prayed, "My Father, if it is not possible for this cup to be taken away unless I drink it, may your will be done." 43 When he came back, he again found them sleeping, because their eyes were heavy. 44 So he left them and went away once more and prayed the third time, saying the same thing. 45 Then he returned to the disciples and said to them, "Are you still sleeping and resting? Look, the hour has come, and the Son of Man is delivered into the hands of sinners. 46 Rise! Let us go! Here comes my betrayer!"*

As you read and meditate on these scriptures, think about how you can apply them to your life, family, career, church, etc. You should always pray and these scriptures will guide you as you pray them through.

Watchmen are appointed and called by God — *I appointed watchmen over you and said, 'Listen to the sound of the trumpet!' But you said, 'We will not listen.'* **Jeremiah 6:17 (NIV)**

They are given a burden for prayer. **Luke 18:1 (CEB)** — Jesus told the disciples a parable about their need to pray continuously and not to be discouraged. Then Jesus taught the followers that they should always pray and never lose hope. "Rejoice always, pray without ceasing, give thanks in all circumstances; for this is the will of God in Christ Jesus for you" (1 Thessalonians 5:16-18, ESV)

◈ Alert

Spiritual: discernment — sensitive to God's Will being performed in the Earth

Natural: alert (level of interest in international, national, local government, attentive to pressing issues on the 7 mountains)

The 7 mountains: Religion, family, education, government, media, arts, & business

The task of a modern-day watchman invariably has the goal of being salt and light in an unbelieving world. The watchman should challenge wrong laws, wrong morality, wrong church teaching, wrong leaders — and so on — through prayer and strategic intervention.

Although salt hurts wounds, it also heals and preserves, but if a watchman fails to challenge society he or she is like "worthless salt." Standing in the Gap — In the ancient world of the Bible, cities had walls surrounding them to provide protection from enemies. When the wall was breached, the city was vulnerable to destruction;

the only way to secure it was for people to risk their lives by literally standing in the gap in the wall and fighting the enemy.

Ezekiel 22:30 — And I sought for a man among them who should build up the wall and stand in the breach before me for the land, that I should not destroy it, but I found none.

Watchmen are assigned to certain jurisdictions. Watchmen are placed by God to have jurisdiction (the official power to make legal decisions and judgments) on the seven mountains of influence/ spheres of society/pillars of culture. It's important that practical prophetic intercessors are alert and aware of what is going on globally so that our times of intercession might be intentional. This is where the relationship between prophecy and prayer is prevalent. **Matthew 21:13 (NIV)** — *My house will be called a house of prayer.*

Ephesians 6:18 (NIV) — *And pray in the Spirit on all occasions with all kinds of prayers and requests. With this in mind, be alert and always keep on praying for all the Lord's people.*

Ephesians 4:11-12 (NKJV) — *And He gave some apostles; and some, prophets; and some, evangelists; and some, pastors and teachers; for the perfecting of the saints, for the work of the ministry, for the edifying of the body of Christ*

Prayer

Father, You are great and greatly to be praised! How wonderful are the works of Your hands that You would create me, fashioned after Your likeness. I thank You, Lord, for wiring me with the capability to have spiritual discernment. I humbly ask that You would activate now in the name of Jesus a deeper level of discernment to be at work within me, being sensitive to God's Will being performed in the earth in the name of Jesus. Guide me to the industries of influence where You have destined me to have impact for Your glory and when I shall arrive and appear in that set place, teach me how to pray, cover, watch over these spears of influence [faith, family, education, government, media, arts and business]. I declare according to Psalm 24:1 NIV, "The earth is the LORD's, and everything in it, the world, and all who live in it." In Jesus' name, Amen.

Reflect and write what the Lord is sharing with you during your time of prayer.

_____

_____

_____

_____

_____

_____

_____

_____

_____

_____

_____

_____

_____

_____

_____

_____

_____

_____

_____

_____

_____

_____

_____

_____

NOTES

What to Expect as a Watchman

A watchman's primary duty is to thwart illegal activity at his employer's property, keeping "whom or what you cover" from harm. They are continually engaged in spiritual warfare (**Ephesians 6:12 AM**P) — *For our struggle is not against flesh and blood [contending only with physical opponents], but against the rulers, against the powers, against the world forces of this [present] darkness, against the spiritual forces of wickedness in the heavenly (supernatural) places.* **Psalm 144:1 (NLT)** — *Praise the LORD, who is my rock. He trains my hands for war and gives my fingers skill for battle.*

Watchmen are given **Privileged Information** — watchmen will be aware of people, situations, events before most people are made aware. (Amos 3:7 — Surely, the Sovereign LORD does nothing without revealing his plan to his servants the prophets). They take **Shelter** in the Father as their place of refuge during prayer— Proverbs 18:10 — The name of the LORD is a strong tower; the righteous man runs into it and is safe. (Also see Psalm 91). **Shared Responsibility** is also something that can be expected as a watchman — **Luke 2:8 (AMPC)** — A*nd in that vicinity there were shepherds living [out under the open sky] in the field, watching [in shifts] over their flock by night.* This shows us that watchmen must have their own community of support. No watchman, prophetic intercessor, should ever be alone.

Prayer

Lord, Your Word says in Ephesians 6:12 AMP — For our struggle is not against flesh and blood [contending only with physical opponents], but against the rulers, against the powers, against the world forces of this [present] darkness, against the spiritual forces of wickedness in the heavenly (supernatural) places. Lord, I lift the shield of faith against all the fiery darts of the enemy and take in my hand the sword of the spirit, the Word of God, and use Your Word against all the forces of evil; and I put on this armor and live and pray in complete dependence upon You, my Great Defender, Protector. Your Word says in Exodus 15:3 NIV, "The Lord is a warrior; the LORD is His name!" You're such a Great Warrior, no weapon formed against us will prosper, God's people are undefeated, and I am victorious through Christ our Lord! I fight the good fight of faith, I persevere, I watch and pray, I lay hold to the horns of the altar until my change has come! I declare every spiritual battle yields to my victory in Christ Jesus! I prophetically declare, this fight is already fixed and won! In Jesus' name, Amen.

Reflect and write what the Lord is sharing with you during your time of prayer.

_____

_____

_____

_____

_____

_____

_____

_____

_____

_____

_____

_____

_____

_____

_____

_____

_____

_____

_____

_____

_____

_____

_____

_____

NOTES

Understanding Your Role as a Watchman

In summary, watchmen are God authorized, legal guardians over the affairs of the Earth. Intercessors are guardians and guards. Where are watchmen assigned? Watchmen are placed by God to have jurisdiction (the official power to make legal decisions and judgments) on the seven mountains of influence/spheres of society/ pillars of culture. It's important that practical prophetic intercessors are alert and aware of what is going on globally so that our times of intercession might be intentional.

Jehovah's Jurisdictional Power

Genesis 1:28 (AMP) — *And God blessed them [granting them certain authority] and said to them, "Be fruitful, multiply, and fill the earth, and subjugate it [putting it under your power]; and rule over (dominate) the fish of the sea, the birds of the air, and every living thing that moves upon the earth."*

Acts 1:8 (AMP) — *"But you will receive power and ability when the Holy Spirit comes upon you; and you will be My witnesses [to tell people about Me] both in Jerusalem and in all Judea, and Samaria, and even to the ends of the earth."*

Jehovah's Jurisdictional Power

Luke 10:19 (NIV) — *I have given you authority to trample on snakes and scorpions and to overcome all the power of the enemy; nothing will harm you.*

Deuteronomy 8:18 (KJV) — *But thou shalt remember the Lord thy God: for it is he that giveth thee power to get wealth, that he may establish his covenant which he swears unto thy fathers, as it is this day.*
- God desires to prosper the intercessor.

Trademarks of a Watchman — Strategic Viewpoint

The watchman stood at the place in the city where he would have the most strategic view of the surroundings and watch for any approaching enemy army.

Trademarks of a Watchman — Watchmen are intercessors

Intercessors are those who have been called to bring Heaven's agenda into the Earth through partnering with God in prayer. Intercessors are also called to be watchmen on the walls of our families, cities, churches, and regions. Will you say yes to the call?

Trademarks of a Watchman — Skilled Communicator

Watchmen had the responsibility to properly communicate and relay to the people if an enemy was approaching. If the watchman delayed the communication or withheld the insight, lives were lost. Who is dying because you won't say anything about what you see?

Trademarks of a Watchman — Clean and Consecrated

The faithful watchman had clean hands, but the unfaithful watchman had hands that were stained by the blood of victims who died because he didn't warn them. Isaiah compared unfaithful watchmen to blind men, dogs that can't bark, and people who can't stay awake (Isaiah. 56:10)

Trademarks of a Watchman — Called to cover

Peter, James, and John were watchmen for Jesus (Mark 14:32-34). They were assigned to cover and be with Him in His lowest point of purpose. You must know WHO covers you and you too must know who you have been **called to cover.**

Prayer

Father, Your Word declares according to 1 Peter 5:8 (NIV), "Be alert and of sober mind. Your enemy the devil prowls around like a roaring lion looking for someone to devour." As Your divinely called watchman, I declare that my mind, vision, and spirit is alert [quick to notice any unusual and potentially difficult circumstances] in the name of Jesus. I thank You for the grace to be sober — not overcome by fear, anxiety, or overthinking. Lord, help me to maintain my focus, assignment, and purpose always — which is to glorify You, be of edification to the saints and an asset to the world. I will not be distracted by the tactics of the devil nor dismayed by the adversary's attempts to prowl. I close every access point to Satan's prowling concerning my life, family, friends, church, community, city, and region now. I thank You for the hedge of protection and the applied blood of Jesus concerning these things. In Jesus' name, Amen.

Reflect and write what the Lord is sharing with you during your time of prayer.

_____

_____

_____

_____

_____

_____

_____

_____

_____

_____

_____

_____

_____

_____

_____

_____

_____

_____

_____

_____

_____

_____

_____

_____

_____

_____

_____

NOTES

Understanding the Prophetic Role of a Watchman

I wish you could all speak in tongues, but even more I wish you could all prophesy. For prophecy is greater than speaking in tongues, unless someone interprets what you are saying so that the whole church will be strengthened. — **1 Corinthians 14:5 (NLT)**

Each watchman is given a certain grace that allows them to have an advantage over the adversary. I would say that it is cutting edge over any technology that is accessible today. It is a system that God uses to inform His people. Prophets are appointed by God before they are formed in their mothers' wombs. It is the Prophetic Grace.

Surely the Sovereign LORD does nothing without revealing his plan to his servants the prophets. — **Amos 3:7 (NIV)**

As a watchman, there are three goals of the Prophetic: to *have spiritual sight, to hear clearly, and to communicate effectively.* The Call is activated/awakened in those appointed to the Office by the Spirit of God. Once awakened by the Holy Spirit, the spirit of the prophet is connected to the Holy Spirit. Prophets live in spiritual awareness of the Holy Spirit. Prophets are gifted and anointed to receive and interpret divine communication, convey communication to their era/generation, strengthen their gifts with the authority of their words to defeat evil efforts that come to block, pervert, diminish the performance of their words. The words of the prophet align earth with heaven and as a result heaven's mandates are manifested in the earth. Mysteries are unfolded to give chronological and/or geographic order. The purpose of prophetic intercession and/or intervention reflects a spiritual transaction to change a situation or circumstance.

The prophetic mantle is devoted to serve and honor Him only. The mantle imparts the ability to effectively hear, see (seer anointing) discern and communicate in the spirit. The seven spirits are before the throne of God (Rev 1:4). These are believed to be the same seven spirits referred to in Isaiah 11:2. Jesus Christ "holds" the seven spirits of God as stated in Rev 3:1. The seven spirits of God are linked with the seven burning lamps that are before God's throne in Rev 4:5. The seven spirits of God are identified in Rev 5:6 with the "seven eyes" of the Lamb and states that they are "sent out into all the earth." The spirit of the prophet is sensitive to and is appropriately empowered by the seven spirits of the Lord.

The Sevenfold Ministry of the Lord:

1. The Spirit of the LORD

2. The Spirit of wisdom

3. The Spirit of understanding

4. The Spirit of counsel

5. The Spirit of strength

6. The Spirit of knowledge

7. The Spirit of the fear of the LORD

These aren't seven distinct Spirits, but one Holy Spirit in His seven-fold activity. In conjunction with the Holy Spirit, a watchman must grow in the fruits of the spirit and continue in the development of Godly character.

Foundational Building Blocks for Prophetic Intercession

• It is okay to learn how to flow prophetically. The disciples even requested that Jesus teach them how to pray (Luke 11:1).

• Remember to use and understand your jurisdictional power to make legal spiritual decisions to loose or bind (Matthew 18:18), declarations (Job 22:28), petitions (Philippians 4:7), adoration (Psalm 33:1)

• We prophesy in proportion to our faith (Romans 12:6); build a well of the Word inside of you to draw from in intercession

How to intertwine prophecy, prayer and scripture

During your meditation/devotion time, settle on a scripture in alignment with your spirit (God will begin to stir one or more of the portals of communication after settling on a scripture to meditate on and intercede.)

• Explore different translations and versions, for example (see below)

Psalm 36:8-9 (NIV) — *They feast on the abundance of your house; you give them drink from your river of delights. For with you is the fountain of life; in your light we see light.*

Psalm 36:8-9 (TPT) — *All may drink of the anointing from the abundance of your house. All may drink their fill from the delightful springs of Eden. 9 To know you is to experience a flowing fountain, drinking in your life, springing up to satisfy. In your light we receive the light of revelation.*

Study to determine the tone of the text (what's going on in the surrounding scriptures, what's the situation at hand, is there tension or pressure?) Study to determine the theological theme in the scripture (what's the characteristic of God being exemplified, is a name of God being demonstrated?) Make mention of keywords in the scripture that can help you create prophetic paths in prayer. It is okay to look up and use synonyms for keywords to help build your path in prayer. Be sensitive to the promptings of the Holy Ghost in prayer.

Isaiah 57:14 (NIV)

And it will be said: "Build up, build up, prepare the road! Remove the obstacles out of the way of my people."

- Tone: Healing, restoration, deliverance/breakthrough, renaissance, reconstruction, repentance
- Theological theme: Mercy, grace, forgiveness, breakthrough, Healer,

Philippians 4:6 (NIV)

Do not be anxious about anything, but in every situation, by prayer and petition, with thanksgiving, present your requests to God.

- Tone: anxiety (worry, stressed, anxious, nervous, fear)
- Theological theme: El Shama – the God who hears and listens, thanksgiving, invitation to present our case to God

2 Corinthians 9:10-11 (NIV)

And [God] Who provides seed for the sower and bread for eating will also provide and multiply your [resources for] sowing and increase the fruits of your righteousness [which manifests itself in active goodness, kindness, and charity].11 Thus you will be enriched in all things and in every way, so that you can be generous, and [your generosity as it is] administered by us will bring forth thanksgiving to God.

- Tone: seasons, sowing,
- Theological theme: Jehovah Jireh (Our provider), generosity, thanksgiving, abundance (abundant supply), Giver/giving

Prayer

Father, our finite human minds cannot fathom Your vault of goodness. In the treasury of Your goodness, I discover Your gifts. Lord, I embrace fully the gift to prophesy. Your Word declares in Numbers 11:29, "...you desire that all the LORD's people were prophets and that the LORD would put his Spirit on them!" Lord, pour out a fresh anointing on me, Your watchman on the wall. Stir up the gift within me for prophetic sight, to hear Your voice ever so clear and to communicate what You speak to me. In the name of Jesus, Amen!

Reflect and write what the Lord is sharing with you during your time of prayer.

_____

_____

_____

_____

_____

_____

_____

_____

_____

_____

_____

_____

_____

_____

_____

_____

_____

_____

_____

_____

_____

_____

_____

_____

_____

NOTES

Understanding the Prophetic World

God shall give you great signs and peaks into what lies ahead! What is God saying? Is God speaking right now? How is He relaying the message? God desires to interject His voice in our lives to give clarity, answers, and guidance; through the communication technology of prophecy – God is also going to edify, exhort and empower you bringing you into a deeper understanding of how the prophetic world works and how to live in it daily. In our church ID statement, we say that we are an apostolic and prophetic epicenter; we also say because we are a people of prayer, by the result we are prophetic, and God's presence is always here – what does that mean and what should that also mean for you?

1 Corinthians 14:24-25 AMP

24 But if all prophesy [foretelling the future, speaking a new message from God to the people], and an unbeliever or outsider comes in, he is convicted [of his sins] by all, and he is called to account by all [because he can understand what is being said]; 25 the secrets of his heart are laid bare. And so, falling on his face, he will worship God, declaring that God is really among you.

John 4:48 NIV

"Unless you people see signs and wonders," Jesus told him, "You will never believe."

Sign Language

One of the greatest quests you'll have in this life is the revelation of God's veracity (truth, accuracy, reality). One of the ways we discover God, come into the knowledge of God, and experience God is through His various forms of communication. The God in Whom we serve is a masterful communicator. He is not mute, thoughtless, or even inaccessible. One of the first acts we see in Genesis between God and man is the two having a conversation in Genesis 2. God is so committed to properly communicating with His people; God has never allowed the progression of time, people, and even Satan himself to prevent Him from using whatever means necessary to relay a message to His own. God is so devoted to communicating with you that He will use signs, wonders, visuals, His Word, and words; one of the technologies that God uses to communicate with man is through prophecy. We don't prophesy out of our own will, imagination, or own inspiration but strictly from God's divine pool of wisdom and insight.

Key: God's Word is prophetic because His Word is potent (having great power, influence, or effect; having or wielding force, authority, or influence: powerful. 2: achieving or bringing about a particular result: effective.)

What is prophecy?

A discourse emanating from divine inspiration and declaring the purposes of God, whether by reproving and admonishing the wicked, comforting the afflicted, revealing hidden things; or foretelling future events.

Prophecy reveals the future — When you hear the purpose of prophecy, it reveals the future. You must understand the times we are living in.

Prophecy prepares — prophecy is the rehearsal of the future to the present. Without prophecy, people do not know nor will prepare for what is coming. Prophecy prepares us for the future. The ultimate purpose of prophecy is for us to be ready for the second coming of Jesus.

2 Peter 1:21 TPT — *No true prophecy comes from human initiative but is inspired by the moving of the Holy Spirit upon those who spoke the message that came from God.*

Some individuals' mental thought and belief have literally choked their faith causing them to believe or perceive that speaking tongues and prophecy ceased with the first Apostolic age we read about in the book of Acts. It is called Cessationism, which is the view that the "miracle gifts" of tongues and healing have ceased—that the end of the apostolic age brought about a cessation of the miracles associated with that age. Most cessationists believe that, while God can and still does perform miracles today, the Holy Spirit no longer uses individuals to perform miraculous signs through tongues and/or prophecy. However, that is not true; three reasons how we know that **prophecy is real and necessary are:**

Acts 2:17-18 (NIV) — In the last days, God says, "I will pour out my Spirit on all people. Your sons and daughters will prophesy, your young men will see visions, your old men will dream dreams. Even on My menservants and maidservants, I will pour out My Spirit in those days, and they will prophesy."

1 Corinthians 14:5 (ESV) — Now I want you all to speak in tongues, but even more to prophesy. The one who prophesies is greater than the one who speaks in tongues, unless someone interprets, so that the church may be built up.

1 Corinthians 14:3 (NIV) — But he who prophesies speaks to men for their edification, encouragement, and comfort.

Revelation 19:10 (NKJV) — …For the testimony of Jesus is the spirit of prophecy.

Ephesians 4:11 (NLT) — Now these are the gifts Christ gave to the church: the apostles, the prophets, the evangelists, and the pastors and teachers.

1 Thess. 5:10 teaches us to despise not prophesying. God inspired the prophet Amos to write, "Surely the Lord GOD does nothing, unless He reveals His secret to His servants the prophets" (Amos 3:7).

Without the presence of communication, we would lie in an abyss of confusion, uncertainty, and even ignorance. Communication is simply the act of transferring information from one place, person, or group to another. The reason why God uses various forms of communication including prophecy is that God uses it as a sign – that He is God. Some people need a SIGN from God that God is alert, aware, and attentive.

1 Corinthians 14:24-25 (AMP)

24 But if all prophesy [foretelling the future, speaking a new message from God to the people], and an unbeliever or outsider comes in, he is convicted [of his sins] by all, and he is called to account by all [because he can understand what is being said]; 25 the secrets of his heart are laid bare. And so, falling on his face, he will worship God, declaring that God is really among you.

Why is prophecy important?

1 Corinthians 14:3 (NIV) — But he who prophesies speaks to men for their **edification, exhortation, and comfort.**

> **Edification** — means to BUILD. The acting of building, whether new or to renew or restore. To promote. 1 Thes. 5:11 teaches us to build one another up…

Isaiah 41:10 (NLT) — Don't be afraid, for I am with you. Don't be discouraged, for I am your God. I will strengthen you and help you. I will hold you up with my victorious right hand.

> Exhortation — to call or summons; to import (to bring something in from another place to this place) You can call things in prophetically (healing, finances, resources, etc.); prophecy is

a form of IMPORT or impartation. Through prophecy refreshing is released to God's people (Ezekiel 37:4).

Romans 4:17 (NKJV) — (as it is written, "I have made you a father of many nations") in the presence of Him whom he believed—God, who gives life to the dead and calls those things which do not exist as though they did.

> Comfort — God uses prophecy as wind to confirm; it breathes life on what's in your spirit to stay alive and continue in hope; it becomes Rhema and real to you! God uses prophecy to quicken the dead, awaken slumbering believers to action and mobility, console, and comfort.

Joshua 1:5-9 (MSG):

"Moses my servant is dead. Get going. Cross this Jordan River, you and all the people. Cross to the country I'm giving to the People of Israel. I'm giving you every square inch of the land you set your foot on—just as I promised Moses. From the wilderness and this Lebanon east to the Great River, the Euphrates River—all the Hittite country—and then west to the Great Sea. It's all yours. All your life, no one will be able to hold out against you. In the same way, I was with Moses, I'll be with you. I won't give up on you; I won't leave you. Strength! Courage! You are going to lead these people to inherit the land that I promised to give their ancestors. Give it everything you have, heart and soul. Make sure you carry out The Revelation that Moses commanded you, every bit of it. Don't get off track, either left or right, so as to make sure you get to where you're going. And don't for a minute let this Book of The Revelation be out of mind. Ponder and meditate on it day and night, making sure you practice

everything written in it. Then you'll get where you're going; then you'll succeed. Haven't I commanded you? Strength! Courage! Don't be timid; don't get discouraged. God, your God, is with you every step you take."

Watchmen are placed by God to have jurisdiction (the official power to make legal decisions and judgments) on the seven mountains of influence/spheres of society/pillars of culture. It's important that practical prophetic intercessors are alert and aware of what is going on globally so that our times of intercession might be intentional.

Luke 18:1 (NKJV) — *that men always ought to pray and not loose heart*

1 Corinthians 14:5 (NIV) — *I would like every one of you to speak in tongues, but I would rather have you prophesy*

Amos 3:7 (NKJV) — *Surely, the Lord God does nothing, unless He reveals His secret to His servants the prophets.*

Matthew 21:13 (NIV) — *My house will be called a house of prayer.*

Ephesians 6:18 (NIV) — *And pray in the Spirit on all occasions with all kinds of prayers and requests. With this in mind, be alert and always keep on praying for all the Lord's people.*

Ephesians 4:11-12 (NKJV) — *And He gave some apostles; and some, prophets; and some, evangelists; and some, pastors and* *teachers; for the perfecting of the saints, for the   work of the ministry, for the edifying of the body of Christ*

Purpose of the Prophet

To stand as the mouth of God in the Earth

• The office of the prophet must never be vacant in the Earth

• It is the office that syncs the Church with what the King is saying; where the word of a king is there is power (Eccl. 8:4)

• Prophet is a very significant gift that must not be muzzled in the House of God. (Deuteronomy 25:4)

Climates for Prophets

Prophetic people are very sensitive to atmospheres. Atmospheres either suffocate or liberate the prophetic.

• Prophets/prophetically graced people thrive in climates saturated in prayer.

• The atmosphere of faith activates gifts and releases a surge of power to prophesy.

• Romans 12:6 – we prophesy according to the proportion of our faith.

• The only way that prophets can be powerful is if there is a consistent stream of revelation released in the House

You Can Reveal it to Me!

Amos 3:7 (NLT) — *Indeed, the Sovereign Lord never does anything until he reveals his plans to his servants the prophets.*

Amos is an advocate, and he is a great Biblical source of light for all who wander in the world of feeling inadequate of being used by God and feeling worthy of having an intimate relationship with God. Amos was not a prophet by vocation; he was a sheep breeder (Amos 1:1).

Amos was not the son of a prophet, didn't come from prophetic people — God chose him and elected him to the prophetic ministry. Amos was content looking after figs and flocks, but God took him from the flock and commanded him to prophesy to Israel. (Amos 7:15). It is during this time in the book of Amos, Samaria, the capital city of Israel, experienced wealth, and luxury; however, this was accompanied by idolatry and moral decline. Amos cried out, prophesying against Samaria's wickedness and self-indulgence.

Amos was tasked to prophesy to people who appeared to be experiencing kingdom blessings: But God had a message for them: prosperity does not imply kingdom blessing when it is mixed with rebellion against Him. These people were enjoying the benefits of prosperity while ignoring the disenfranchised among them. **Amos was very direct in telling the people they could not enjoy kingdom benefits without living kingdom lives.** Amos shows how God uses those living under his kingdom plan to accomplish his promises of blessings. Amos had a serious responsibility of communicating this message to Israel. It involved not only Israel's spiritual condition, but God layered his assignment to also go into the economy and government. *Isaiah has told us in Isaiah 43:19 KJV, Behold, I will do a new thing; now it shall spring forth; shall ye not know it? I will even make a way in the wilderness, and rivers in the desert.*

Meaning, that God is just not raising up prophetic voices in the four walls of the church – God is raising up prophetic people who can be trusted with sensitive information with people of influence in 7 mountains of influence: media, government, education, economy, family, religion, arts/entertainment. God needs a voice He can use!

He used Daniel to speak prophetically to King Nebuchadnezzar, He used Prophetess Esther to speak prophetically to the king, He used Prophet Moses to speak prophetically to Pharaoh! It's rare that you see prophetic people locked and limited to only people of faith! *Prophetic people are the voice of God in places of influence!*

Prophetic people are called to be trustworthy people. Prophecy is not a "performance gift" but prophecy is a place and time of intimate conversation between the celestial and terrestrial; the mortal and the immortal; the supernatural and the natural; between humanity and divinity.

To view prophecy as only telling the future is short-changing the power of prophecy. **Prophecy is powered via intimacy with God.** Anything revealed to you outside of an intimate relationship with God is called divination. Divination is - Attempts to discover the unknown or the future by involving communication with the spirit world. It is expressly forbidden by God and has disastrous consequences. Retrieving information, around God, ignoring God.

I have learned in life, and it's my prayer that mature adults are aware of this as well — it takes time to build trust with people, especially with sensitive information. We should be swift with our trust towards and with God and cautious with our trust with man. Certain matters in our lives, I just must take to God and leave it there; in addition to, God will surround you with godly men and women who live integral, trustworthy lives that are able to handle given information. Often, people are left in a world warring with their own thoughts because they have been burned so many times with loose-mouth people who had not proven over time their maturity — *"If it's not your story to tell, you don't tell it."* — *Iyanla Vanzant.*

Indeed, the Sovereign Lord never does anything until he reveals his plans to his servants the prophets.

One key part in this text, I want us to observe today is – the LORD never does anything until He reveals his **plans**...*you can reveal it to me! His plans are on the other side of the prophetic. God's plans for our lives are revealed in the intimate place. Apostle, how do I get the plans?*
Plans in Hebrew is SODE (H5475) — familiar converse, intimacy with God, **in close deliberation.**

Out of familiar conversation, friendly, intimate, transparent, vulnerable dialogue with God will result in plans being revealed! Jesus demonstrates this in **Matthew 16:19-20 (NLT)** — *"And I will give you the keys of the Kingdom of Heaven. Whatever you forbid on earth will be forbidden in heaven, and whatever you permit on earth* *will be permitted in heaven."* ***Then he sternly warned the disciples not to tell anyone that he was the Messiah.***

What you're looking for, what you need, the answers you are yearning for, the vision of the Lord is yoked up in intimacy with Him. Secrets are revealed in the intimate place with you and God, and it's prophetic. Get out of everybody's prophetic line for a Word and get on your knees, ask God to give you a tarry (waiting language) to get the revelation you need!

Did you know that being prophetic allows you to have in-close deliberation with God?

Deliberation is - long and careful consideration or discussion, long and careful consideration or discussion.

Biblically, this proves to us that you and God can become so close, intimate that the two of you can deliberate on the affairs and matters of this life.

Job 22:28 — *You will decide on a matter, and it will be established for you, and light will shine on your ways.*

Deuteronomy 29:29 NLT — *The Lord our God has secrets known to no one. We are not accountable for them, but we and our children are accountable forever for all that he has revealed to us, so that we may obey all the terms of these instructions.*

Spirit of the Lord is speaking to those who are in a decision-making season – your biggest place of warfare will be in your place of intimacy; intimacy reveals the plans of God!

Remember in **Amos 3:3 NLT**, *can two people walk together without agreeing on the direction?* This is an amazing scripture to structure our platonic relationships around, but this has nothing to do with earthly man-to-man relationships. This is a prophetic rhetorical question. This scripture is about God and man walking together – without you agreeing with God on the same direction, you'll get nowhere.

Prophecy reveals the heart (intents, thoughts, decisions of God) and deposits them into the heart of man. But can God trust you with his revelations?

Jonah ran away from the revelations; John shaped his lifestyle around what God showed him. It's impossible to be intimate with GOD and not be used by him. Everyone that was close to Jesus was used by Jesus.

For those who can commit to becoming more intimate with Jesus like never before — you'll come into a prophetic place where plans are revealed such as what was revealed in **Amos 9:13-15 MSG:** *"Yes indeed, it won't be long now." God's Decree. "Things are going to happen so fast your head will swim, one thing fast on the heels of the other. You won't be able to keep up. Everything will be happening at once—and everywhere you look blessings! Blessings like wine pouring off the mountains and hills. I'll make everything right again for my people Israel: They'll rebuild their ruined cities. They'll plant vineyards and drink good wine They'll work their gardens and eat fresh vegetables. And I'll plant them, plant them on their own land. They'll never again be uprooted from the land I've given them. God, your God, says so."*

Prophetic Intercession Culture

Weeping and wailing prayer

• Power of tears (Psalm 42:3, Hebrew 5:7, Luke 7:44)

• Power of brokenness (psalm 51)

• Dimension of repentance and forgiveness

• Tongues and Groaning (Romans 8:26, Proverbs 25:2, 1 Corinthians 14:2)

• Travail and birthing (Galatians 4:19)

• Mysteries revealed and revelation unlocked (1 Corinthians 14:2)

• Deliverance (Psalm 31)

• Declarations and Decrees

• Judgements (1 Corinthians 7:25)

• Alignments (James 4:4)

• Prophetic decrees (Romans 4:17)

Romans 4:17 (NLT) — *That is what the Scriptures mean when God told him, "I have made you the father of many nations." This hap-*

pened because Abraham believed in the God who brings the dead back to life and who creates new things out of nothing.

Dual Roles of Responsibilities of Prophets & Intercessors

• Called to a lifestyle of holiness (character, spiritual maturity, discipline, seasoned appetite for the Word, intercession)

• Prayer — An important part of the prophets' task is prayer. They have a clear picture of what God is doing, so he knows where prayer is needed most. The prophets watch over the word of the Lord and pray it into being. They must not rest until God has fulfilled his word (Isaiah 62:6).

• Operate in jurisdictional prophetic power in prayer Dual Roles of Responsibilities of Prophets & Intercessors

• A key role of the prophet is waiting in the presence of God to receive the word of God. God is sovereign, so we cannot tell him when he should speak. Hearing will always require waiting.

• Prophetic people experience levels of suffering. Deep dealing at the hand of God will often be needed to prepare the prophet for receiving the word of God. Sometimes we may actually have to experience beforehand, something of what his people will experience.

• Worship

• Interpreting seasons and times How God Communicates

• Prayer is diplomatic power (skill of managing international relations [kingdoms], the practice of conducting negotiations between heaven and earth, it entails influencing the decisions)

How God Communicates

• Prayer is negotiating power.

• Prayer is the only LEGAL way anything from heaven has authority to enter the Earth.

> **Matthew 18:18 (AMP)** — *I assure you and most solemnly say to you, whatever you bind [forbid, declare to be improper and unlawful] on earth shall have [already] been bound in heaven, and whatever you loose [permit, declare lawful] on earth [b]shall have [already] been loosed in heaven.*

Legal ways to use prayer:

• Petition the Father

• Gain access to the supernatural (open heaven and revelation)

• Receive gifts

• Stretch capacity of gifts, anointing, and rank

• Shift wills (not my will)

• The passageway to hear, see and experience how God Communicates

• God is Spirit (John 4:24), therefore He requires human communication to be hosted in a spiritual vehicle which is prayer.

• God's official form of communication is prayer.

• Prophetic prayer is communicating God's Word back to Him; His Word adds speed to the spiritual vehicle (prayer).

• Prophetic prayer is communicating God's Word back to Him:
> **Isaiah 62:6 (AMPC)**:
> *I have set watchmen upon your walls, O Jerusalem, who will never hold their peace day or night; you who [are His servants and by your prayers] put the Lord in remembrance [of His promises], keep not silence,*

His Word adds speed to the spiritual vehicle (prayer):
> *a.* **Jeremiah 1:12 (AMPC)** — *Then said the Lord to me, You have seen well, for I am alert and active, watching over My word to perform it.*
> *b.* **Isaiah 55:11 (NLT)** — *It is the same with my word. I send it out, and it always produces fruit. It will accomplish all I want it to, and it will prosper everywhere I send it.*

His Word adds speed to the spiritual vehicle (prayer):

c. **Numbers 23:19 (NIV)** — *God is not a man, that He should lie, or a son of man, that He should change His mind. Does He speak and not act? Does He promise and not fulfill?*

d. **Ezekiel 24:14 (NIV)** — *I the LORD have spoken. The time has come for me to act.*

e. **Job 22:28 (KJV)** — *Thou shalt also decree a thing, and it shall be established unto thee: and the light shall shine upon thy ways.*

Adding Prophetic Speed to Your Prayers

1. Pray God's Word.

2. Pray God's Will.

3. Declare timing.

4. Wait on God. **Acts 4:30-32 (NKJV):**

"By stretching out Your hand to heal, and that signs and wonders may be done through the name of Your holy Servant Jesus." 31 And when they had prayed, the place where they were assembled together was shaken; and they were all filled with the Holy Spirit, and they spoke the word of God with boldness.

Adding Prophetic Speed to Your Prayers

Luke 9:29 (NIV) — *As he was praying, the appearance of his face changed, and his clothes became as bright as a flash of lightning.*

Luke 3:21 (NLT) — *One day when the crowds were being baptized, Jesus himself was baptized. As he was praying, the heavens opened.*

Reflect and write what the Lord is sharing with you during your time of prayer.

_____

_____

_____

_____

_____

_____

_____

_____

_____

_____

_____

_____

_____

_____

_____

_____

_____

_____

_____

_____

_____

_____

_____

_____

NOTES

Trust the Prophetic Process

Helping believers to identify the stages of a prophetic word and how to respond to the stages.

Luke 1:5-20 NLT: *[5] When Herod was king of Judea, there was a Jewish priest named Zechariah. He was a member of the priestly order of Abijah, and his wife, Elizabeth, was also from the priestly line of Aaron. [6] Zechariah and Elizabeth were righteous in God's eyes, careful to obey all of the Lord's commandments and regulations. [7] They had no children because Elizabeth was unable to conceive, and they were both very old.*

[8] One day Zechariah was serving God in the Temple, for his order was on duty that week. [9] As was the custom of the priests, he was chosen by lot to enter the sanctuary of the Lord and burn incense. [10] While the incense was being burned, a great crowd stood outside, praying.

[11] While Zechariah was in the sanctuary, an angel of the Lord appeared to him, standing to the right of the incense altar. [12] Zechariah was shaken and overwhelmed with fear when he saw him. [13] But the angel said, "Don't be afraid, Zechariah! God has heard your prayer. Your wife, Elizabeth, will give you a son, and you are to name him John. [14] You will have great joy and gladness, and many will rejoice at his birth, [15] for he will be great in the eyes of the Lord. He must never touch wine or other alcoholic drinks. He will be

filled with the Holy Spirit, even before his birth. [16] And he will turn many Israelites to the Lord their God. [17] He will be a man with the spirit and power of Elijah. He will prepare the people for the coming of the Lord. He will turn the hearts of the fathers to their children, and he will cause those who are rebellious to accept the wisdom of the godly."

[18] Zechariah said to the angel, "How can I be sure this will happen? I'm an old man now, and my wife is also well along in years."

[19] Then the angel said, "I am Gabriel! I stand in the very presence of God. It was he who sent me to bring you this good news! [20] But now, since you didn't believe what I said, you will be silent and unable to speak until the child is born. ***For my words will certainly be fulfilled at the proper time."***

It is common that most believers receive a prophetic word at some point and time in your walk with God. The prophetic word often reveals an expected end as Jeremiah would say in Jeremiah 29:11 that God desires to progress you to. Receiving a prophetic word concerning future successes, family establishment, career advancements, ministry ambitions revealed – all of those are wonderful, but no prophetic word will produce, come alive, manifest lest it goes through the necessary process for manifestation. A process is a series of actions or steps taken to achieve a particular end. Today's lesson is to help believers identify the stages of a prophetic word and how to respond to the stages thereof.

A process is a course that is essential for progression. All prophecies come with a process; a prophetic word is not going to just manifest because it has your name on it. You cannot see the promised *thing* without the process attached to it – the process is indispensable, and it will include your involvement! There are some key areas of involvement in the stages that we must address today to help you get to the prophetic promises God has made concerning you!

The prophetic process, the process that starts with revelation from the heart of God, and finishes, hopefully, with fulfillment and transformation. **Prophecy is not a one-time event, but rather a long-term process, as we align our lives and properly walk out the word from God.** To have a prophetic lifestyle – and to be a disciple of Jesus — involves engaging with the whole of this process.

In our text, Luke introduces his readers to Zechariah and his wife Elizabeth who were from the tribe of Levi and descended from Moses's brother Aaron. Thus, Zechariah was a priest. According to 1 Chronicles 24:7-18, the temple priests were divided into 24 divisions. Each division would serve for two weeks a year at the temple in Jerusalem.

Zechariah and Elizabeth were faithful, elderly followers of God. Nevertheless, they were childless because Elizabeth had never been able to conceive.

One unique occasion when it was Zechariah's turn to serve; the Bible said he was chosen by lot to serve, it was his time to serve. But not only was it his time to serve, it was his turn for something supernatural. I'd like to add a footnote here to never underestimate the power of serving or take it for granted — something supernatural can happen while you're serving! **God works through seemingly random processes to accomplish His will.**

11 While Zechariah was in the sanctuary, an angel of the Lord appeared to him, standing to the right of the incense altar. [12] Zechariah was shaken and overwhelmed with fear when he saw him. [13] But the angel said, "Don't be afraid, Zechariah! God has heard your prayer. Your wife, Elizabeth, will give you a son, and you are to name him John.

VISITATION

Key: A prophetic word first begins with an experience or an encounter. (vs. 11-13)

Authentic prophetic moments are birthed out of times of worship, prayer/intercession or God may even meet you while you're serving. Zechariah's prophetic moment happened while He was serving, and God sent an angel to relay a prophetic message.

AUTHENTICATION

Key: Prophetic words will *always* encompass the purposes of God.

[15] for he will be great in the eyes of the Lord. He must never touch wine or other alcoholic drinks. He will be filled with the Holy Spirit, even before his birth. [16] And he will turn many Israelites to the Lord their God. [17] He will be a man with the spirit and power of Elijah. He will prepare the people for the coming of the Lord. He will turn the hearts of the fathers to their children and he will cause those who are rebellious to accept the wisdom of the godly."

When God gives you a prophetic word, it will be tailored to bless you, it's for your good, it's in our favor but it's always ultimately for the glory of God. Given Zechariah's age, this would be miraculous for them to bear a child at this stage in their lives. It was more than just blessing them with a child. This child would grow to be a major role in God's kingdom's plans for salvation and redemption.

Here's where we gain deeper insight in our lesson of recognizing the prophetic process God sends us through — after I have an encounter/experience and gain revelation of the prophecy,

PREPARATION

After you've had a visitation (encounter or experience), your experience is authenticated, next is preparation for what has been revealed! The Bible says, [18] Zechariah said to the angel, "How can I be sure this will happen? I'm an old man now, and my wife is also well along in years."

Despite the angel's words, Zechariah didn't believe. How could it be possible? Zechariah was full of doubt. **Your faith can move mountains, but your doubt can create them.** You must have faith; faith is a key part, a major part of the process! You can't see, achieve, or receive without faith! Faith is our positive response to what God has already provided. Now here are three key areas of your faith you must develop in a prophetic process:

Patience — faith, and patience are power twins.
<u>Hebrews 6:12 MSG</u> — *And now I want each of you to extend that same intensity toward a full-bodied hope and keep at it till the finish. Don't drag your feet. Be like those who stay the course with committed faith and then get everything promised to them.*

Hebrews 6:12 ICB — We do not want you to become lazy. Be like those who have faith and patience. They will receive what God has promised.

You can't understand patience without properly understanding time. Ecclesiastes 3:1, to everything there is a season, an appointed time; the Bible declares, when the time was right, God sent His Son Jesus (Gal. 4:4); there is a set time for the Word of the Lord to come to past. But we must be patient.

Prayer — **Matthew 21:22 NLT** — *"You can pray for anything, and if you have faith, you will receive it."*

Preparation — *"Every word I've spoken to you will come true on time—God's time."* **Luke 1:20 (The Message)**

Being patient doesn't mean that we are idle and do nothing; working is a part of the process. God required Zechariah to be silent because he didn't want his doubt to have any volume. What is God requiring you to do in the process?

If God has spoken it, it will come to past! Luke 1:20 — every word I've spoken will come true on time! How do I know that?

Hebrews 10:23 CEB — Let's hold on to the confession of our hope without wavering, because the one who made the promises is reliable.

Reflect and write what the Lord is sharing with you during your time of prayer.

_____

_____

_____

_____

_____

_____

_____

_____

_____

_____

_____

_____

_____

_____

_____

_____

_____

_____

_____

_____

_____

_____

_____

_____

_____

NOTES

Activating the Gift of the Holy Spirit in Prayer

Acts 2:38 (NKJV)

Then Peter said to them, "Repent, and let every one of you be baptized in the name of Jesus Christ for the remission of sins; and you shall receive the gift of the Holy Spirit."

God is a giver, and He always gives His best. Each member of the Godhead gave His greatest possible gift to humankind. Each gift was given with the same love motivation for the benefit of the one receiving the gift, and it is the best and greatest gift that could possibly be given. The Father's gift of His Son, Jesus was His best gift for the world [John 3:16].

The love of God is a giving love. True divine love gives its best. God the Father so loved...that He gave His only-begotten Son. Jesus was the nearest and dearest to the heart of God. There was not a greater gift from His whole Being and eternal universe that God could give. For God to give Jesus was to give Himself. God's past, present and future was centered in His Son Jesus. Jesus is the fulfillment of all of God's desire and purpose.

Jesus, the Son's gift of the Holy Spirit to the Church was the best gift He could give, and the Holy Spirit's gift of the spiritual language was the best and greatest gift for the individual believer. Acts 2:38 teaches us a precept I want us all to hold on to —

Key: All who REPENT are eligible to RECEIVE the gift of the Holy Spirit.

This divine gift of speaking in an unknown tongue is the divinely given ability to pray in a language that was never learned by natural means. It is an experience received when God baptizes a Christian's redeemed and born-again spirit with the ability to pray in an intelligent language that your natural mind did not learn and does not understand or comprehend. Speaking in tongues is not a naturally learned ability, but a supernaturally imparted ability. It is not emotional gibberish, meaningless sounds, or hollow expressions.

Acts 10:44-46 (NIV)
While Peter was still speaking these words, the Holy Spirit came on all who heard the message. 45 The circumcised believers who had come with Peter were astonished that the gift of the Holy Spirit had been poured out even on Gentiles. 46 For they heard them speaking in tongues and praising God.

—Believing the Word opens up the way for the filling of the Holy Spirit.
—This gift is not reserved for certain people, but this gift is available to all who hunger and thirsts after righteousness

God desires that we *__activate__* [make something operative] crank up, start up, turn on.

In **Mark 16:17 (NKJV)** — *And these signs will follow those who [a]believe: In My name they will cast out demons; they will speak with new tongues;* Jesus tells us about this gift. He lays it out—authority in the unseen spirit realm, authority to operate over demons, and authority to have open access to the realm of the Holy Spirit—to speak with new tongues.

Tongues is the Master Key to operating in the Kingdom in a higher dimension and accessing the ministry of the Holy Spirit. Everything the Spirit does and every way He does it can be touched through tongues. In other words, whatever you need, tongues will guide you to a solution. Here are a few benefits:

Tongues is direct contact with God.
"For he who speaks in a tongue does not speak to men but to God, for no one understands him; however, in the spirit he speaks mysteries." — **1 Corinthians 14:2 (NKJV)**

When you pray in tongues, you are in direct contact with God. It's your own private language with Him that no one else understands because you're speaking to God. It's direct communication between your spirit and God. You're speaking the language only HE understands.

God has given the Church a divine, supernatural means of communication with Him that is so power-packed, we would be missing out if we prayed in our own language alone.

Now, it is important to remember that praying in tongues is NOT meant to replace praying in your known language, but to add to it. We've all experienced times when we've come to the end of what we can accomplish through natural prayer. That's when we move over into tongues.

Praying in the spirit is a divine secret between God and me. It is my future. It is my heritage. It is my destination. It is the vision of my life being prayed out and given root to before it is ever made known to this natural world. **Ephesians 6:18** — *pray in the spirit at all times and on every occasion.*

Tongues remind us of His indwelling presence.

"And I will pray the Father, and he shall give you another Comforter, that he may abide with you forever...for he dwelleth with you, and shall be in you." — **John 14:16-17 (KJV)**

Another power-packed reason to pray in tongues is that it reminds us that the Holy Spirit brings your inner man to life by dwelling inside us every minute of every day. When challenges arise, that reminder will shut down all the outside voices and build our strength to see ourselves as He does—victorious.

Tongues Is for Edification

"He who speaks in a tongue edifies himself." — **1 Corinthians 14:4 (NKJV)**

To edify means build yourself up. Edify, in the Greek translation in 1 Corinthians 14:4 means, "to build a house, to build up from the foundation". I could not resist reflecting on Matthew 7:24-24 where Jesus gave a parable about two people who built houses. One built a house on the Rock, and on built it on sand. Not activating your gift to pray in the Spirit could put you at risk of building relationships, careers, businesses, making commitments and decisions on sand.

Matthew 7:24-27 (ESV) — [24] *"Everyone then who hears these words of mine and does them will be like a wise man who built his house on the rock.* [25] *And the rain fell, and the floods came, and the winds blew and beat on that house, but it did not fall, because it had been founded on the rock.* [26] *And everyone who hears these words of mine and does not do them will be like a foolish man who built his house on the sand.* [27] *And the rain fell, and the floods came, and the winds blew and beat against that house, and it fell, and great was the fall of it."*

In Christ, there is always HOPE! We've all done things we didn't pray in the Spirit about! Good news is, **edify also means to restore by building, to rebuild and to repair.**

Praying in the Spirit activates the restorative work of God to take place in the life of the believer! **Speaking in tongues builds you up to the point that you can believe God instead of circumstances.**

"But you, beloved, building yourselves up on your most holy faith, praying in the Holy Spirit." — **Jude 20 (NKJV)**

We need to continually stir up and stimulate our faith. Praying in tongues is another way to stimulate our faith and stay strong and fresh for battle.

Acts 2:38-39 (NKJV)

Then Peter said to them, "Repent, and let every one of you be baptized in the name of Jesus Christ for the remission of sins; and you shall receive the gift of the Holy Spirit. [39] *For the promise is to you and to your children, and to all who are afar off, as many as the Lord our God will call."*

Prayer is so important because it connects us to the presence of God. But in part, prayer is not just a posture before God, but it is also a place in God. When you pray, you leave fear and go into a place of faith. When you pray, you step out of a world of weariness and enter a place of rest. When you pray, you depart chaos and arrive to a place of peace. **Psalm 61:2 (NIV)**, *"From the ends of the earth I call to you, I call as my heart grows faint; lead me to the rock that is higher than I."* There are entry doors into this realm of the supernatural and the gift of the Holy Spirit is one of those entry points. "Activating the Gift of the Holy Spirit" explains to you the **promise** God has made all believers, the **purpose** of the gift of the Holy Spirit and the **power** of the *gift* of the Holy Spirit.

The Promise

While Jesus was on earth with His disciples, He declared to them in *John 14:16-17, "And I will pray the Father, and He will give you another Helper, that He may abide with you forever— 17 the Spirit of truth, whom the world cannot receive, because it neither sees Him nor knows Him; but you know Him, for He dwells with you and will be in you."*

Jesus revealed that He was going to send the Holy Spirit with a new experience for them: as the Holy Spirit was "with" them now, He would be "in" them then. Just before Jesus ascended to Heaven He told the disciples, *"You shall be baptized with the Holy Spirit not many days from now."* **Acts 1:5**

<u>Key:</u> **The baptism of the Holy Spirit is a promised experience and endowment available to all.**

About 120 of the followers of Jesus, went back to Jerusalem and waited for the promise of the Father, the baptism with the Holy Spirit according to **Acts 1:8**, *"You shall receive power after that the Holy Spirit has come upon you…"*

They gathered in an upper room in Jerusalem to wait for the promise of being baptized with the Holy Spirit. Seven days later, God's appointed time arrived — in the early morning on the day the Jews were celebrating the Feast of Pentecost. As the disciples began praising God that morning, the Holy Spirit suddenly came like a mighty win and with tongues of fire that set the believers' tongues ablaze. They began to speak in unknown tongues as they received the gift of their spirit language.

Jesus made this promise and He fulfilled it. He promised you a gift — **James 1:17 (NIV)** — *very good and perfect gift is from above, coming down from the Father of the heavenly lights, who does not change like shifting shadows.*

God does not renege concerning His promises. One element of faith that you must have it is in God's nature to fulfill His promises. He is the God who keeps His promises. This promise was not for just an exclusive group of followers that were with Jesus — this promise is to the New Testament Church; this promise includes you and me.

Psalm 145:13 (NIV) — *"Your kingdom is an everlasting kingdom, and your dominion endures through all generations. The LORD is trustworthy in all he promises and faithful in all he does."*

Acts 2:39 — *"For the promise is to you and to your children, and to all who are afar off, as many as the Lord our God will call."*

This promise is to you, your children and to all who are afar off [this talks about for people in the future!] This promise is active until the Lord returns! Jesus and Peter declared that the only conditions to receive the gift of the Holy Spirit were to believe and obey. Jesus proclaimed:

John 7:38-39 (AMP): *[38] He who believes in Me [who adheres to, trusts in, and relies on Me], as the Scripture has said, "From his innermost being will flow continually rivers of living water." [39] But He was speaking of the [Holy] Spirit, whom those who believed in Him [as Savior] were to receive afterward. The Spirit had not yet been given, because Jesus was not yet glorified (raised to honor).*

Acts 5:32 (NKJV) — *"And we are His witnesses to these things, and so also is the Holy Spirit whom God has given to those who obey Him."*

The Purpose

God is a Spirit. The Holy Spirit's gift of the spirit language enables the believer to communicate with God directly from spirit to spirit — from your inner spirit being to God who is a Spirit. Those who have been born of the Spirit and baptized with the Spirit receive a spirit language. This gives the believer a private communication line direct to God's throne which cannot be understood or hindered by the devil or natural man. It is like having one's private telephone to Heaven. However, the gift is designed to be used for more than communication to God in prayer.

This gift is the greatest gift a Christian can receive, for it is the giver and operator of all the other gifts and graces of God. The "mother of all miracles" is the gift of the Holy Spirit. The Word declares that the tongue is the most powerful member in the human body. The tongue is so set in the body that it can sanctify the body for God's use or set it on hell's fire for the devil's use. The power of life and death is in the tongue!

Could it be that He fills us with the Holy Ghost so that we can speak and declare life even when we try to speak death over ourselves! When you don't know what to say, pray in the Spirit!

Receiving the baptism of the Holy Spirit is an act of faith! It takes great faith and trust in God to allow Him to have us speak in a heavenly spirit language that our mind does not understand or know what is being spoken.

The Spirit gives you utterance to speak – this gift becomes a permanent capability and characteristic of the new man in Christ. The inner man can speak at will in his spirit language the same as the natural physical man can speak at will in his native learned language.

The Power

Tongues is a weapon for weaknesses.

*"Likewise, the Spirit also helps in our weaknesses. For we do not know what we should pray for as we ought, but the Spirit Himself makes **intercession** for us with groanings which cannot be uttered."* **Romans 8:26 (NKJV)**

The Holy Spirit will help you gain strength in any area where you are weak. You are strong in the Lord and the power of His might! So, whenever you're feeling weak, insufficient, or defeated, pray in tongues. The Holy Spirit is inside you to meet that need.

Intercession in the Hebrew [paga] — means, to strike the mark. When you pray in the Spirit, you *paga*, you address concerns, matters, and issues head-on. There is no, "talking around the bush" or ignoring "the white elephant in the room" when you pray in the Spirit.

> *And the Father who knows all hearts knows what the Spirit is saying, for the Spirit pleads for us believers in harmony with God's own will.* **Romans 8:27 (NLT)**

Tongues is a source of supernatural strength and stamina.

Ephesians 3:16 (NLT) — *I pray that from his glorious, unlimited resources he will empower you with inner strength through his Spirit.*

2 Corinthians 4:16 (NLT) — *That is why we never give up. Though our bodies are dying, our spirits are being renewed every day.*

Tongues birth answers from the inside out.
"For one who speaks in an [unknown] tongue speaks not to men but to God, for no one understands or catches his meaning, because in the [Holy] Spirit he utters secret truths

and hidden things [not obvious to the understanding]." — **1 Corinthians 14:2 (AMPC)**

You are meant to have inside information! And you can. Praying in tongues is how God gets it to you. It is the way we can pray out mysteries, which we also refer to as divine revelation. When you don't know what to do, God will tell you through praying in tongues. Tongues is a mystery master and a problem solver. What kinds of things will He reveal?

- The bottomless things of God (**1 Corinthians 2:9-10**):

- The Word

- Ways of escape

- The Mystery of the Future: *"He will show you things to come."* (**John 16:13, *KJV*)**

- God's plan for your future.

You're never alone. Whenever you need help, the answer is only a prayer away. "Praying in the spirit makes you smarter than yourself."

Praying in the Spirit brings peace!

"I am leaving you with a gift—peace of mind and heart. And the peace I give is a gift the world cannot give. So don't be troubled or afraid." **John 14:27 (NLT)**

Tongues magnify God!

"For they heard them speak with tongues, and magnify God." — **Acts 10:46 (KJV)**

Perhaps of all the power-packed reasons to pray in tongues we've covered today, the most important very well may be that tongues magnifies God. When God becomes bigger—in your eyes, in your mind, in your ministry, in everything in your life—every doubt and fear will disappear, and your faith will abound beyond anything you could have ever imagined. He is worthy to be magnified above all else. O magnify the Lord with me and let us exalt His name together! Let the LORD be magnified who takes pleasure in the prosperity of His servant!

Paul told Timothy, *"Stir up the gift of God which is in you,"* **2 Tim. 1:6**. The Word activate is synonymous with "stir up."

Matthew 6:9-10 NKJV
[9] *In this manner, therefore, pray: Our Father in heaven, Hallowed be Your name.*
[10] *Your kingdom come. Your will be done On earth as it is in heaven.*

The greatest invitation extended to man that is imperishable — is God Himself inviting us to Him. Throughout the scenes of the Scriptures, God is extending an open invitation to us.

Revelation 22:17 (NKJV) — *And the Spirit and the bride say, "Come!" And let him who hears say, "Come!" And let him who thirsts come. Whoever desires, let him take the water of life freely.*

Hebrews 4:16 (NKJV) — *Let us therefore come boldly to the throne of grace, that we may obtain mercy and find grace to help in time of need.*

When an invitation is extended, it means, your presence is requested, the essence of your presence is desired in a certain space. In the manner of proper context tonight, this invitation involves and includes your invitation to commune with God through prayer. Prayer isn't a religious duty but an open invitation for all.

The greatest partnership known to man is God's willingness to partner with us through the means of prayer. God invites us to collaborate with His cause [will] via prayer.

The enemy attempts to shackle and chain God's people in a spirit of fear and intimidation due to ignorance. Even though all have received this open invitation of a direct communication line with God, some battle "fear" concerning prayer and are so intimidated because one may feel as if "they don't know what to say" for God to "approve of" or answer their prayer.

Understand this concept: Just as every industry has special jargon [special words or expressions that are used by a particular group and are difficult for others to understand], so does the Kingdom of God. The Kingdom's jargon is God's Word. When you pray the Word of God, you had weight, substance, and authority to your prayer.

Key: Praying with weight means 'praying God's Word back to Him in faith.'

Prayer links us to a heavenly realm we are unfamiliar navigating. Prayer is the God given communication link between heaven and earth, time and eternity, the finite, and the infinite. Simply put, it is the relational communication with God, but you must pray the Word of God.

Principles:
Praying the Word declares TRUTH over all matters.

Because we live in a broken world due to sin, we all encounter circumstances that are real, but it's not the truth. Truth prevails over reality. Truth supersedes the reality that we often become confined to. What happens within you starts to manifest outside of you; it doesn't have to be in your hand for it to be true!

Proverbs 30:5 (ESV) — *Every word of God proves true; [anything I pray from the Word is the truth.]*

Praying the Word puts everything in alignment with His Will.

1 John 5:14-15 (NIV) — *This is the confidence we have in approaching God: that if we ask anything according to his* *will, he hears us. 15 And if we know that he hears us—whatever we ask—we know that we have what we asked of him.*

Psalm 37:4 (ESV) — *Delight yourself in the LORD, and he will give you the desires of your heart.*

Praying the Word produces confidence in His character.

> **Daniel 3:16-17 (NIV)** *[16] Shadrach, Meshach and Abednego replied to him, "King Nebuchadnezzar, we do not need to defend ourselves before you in this matter." [17] If we are thrown into the blazing furnace, **the God we serve is able to deliver us** from it, and he will deliver us from Your Majesty's hand.*

Praying the Word yields supernatural results.

> **Matthew 8:8 (NIV)** — *The centurion replied, "Lord, I do not deserve to have you come under my roof. But just say the word, and my servant will be healed."*
>
> **James 5:16 (AMPC)** — *The earnest (heartfelt, continued) prayer of a righteous man makes tremendous power available [dynamic in its working].*

Praying the Word activates the prophetic.

<u>Romans 4:17 (KJV)</u> — *calleth those things which be not as though they were.*

Whenever you have a situation or circumstance that needs God's intervention, pray the Word over the matter!

Reflect and write what the Lord is sharing with you during your time of prayer.

_____

_____

_____

_____

_____

_____

_____

_____

_____

_____

_____

_____

_____

_____

_____

_____

_____

_____

_____

_____

_____

_____

_____

_____

_____

NOTES

Functions of a Watchman

Ezekiel 33:7 identifies 3 major functions: watch, hear, speak, and in order to know how to operate in these functions we must understand the watchmen of old. Go with me as well dive deeper into what your role entails.

Israel has always had many enemies (then and now unfortunately) and historically the city of Jerusalem had thick high walls around the entire city. In fact, many great cities in olden days had walls around them for protection. For example, we read in scripture about the walls surrounding Babylon and the great walls of Jericho.

Now Israel's watchmen were guards who would stand upon the walls of Jerusalem and in the towers and lookout upon the land. The Hebrew word for watchman is 'tsaphah' and it has the meaning 'to lean forward, to peer into the distance; by implication means to observe, behold, spy out, wait for, keep the watch.'

So they would be in their towers and upon the walls and would literally be peering forward, looking out into the distance, on the watch for messengers, unusual activity, or mostly importantly, any sign of an enemy or approaching army. A very, very important job! With that in mind, let's have a look at God's assessment of Israel's watchmen in the days of Isaiah.

Two Kinds of Watchmen

First, in an ancient agrarian society, guarding the crops was of supreme importance. In that time, people by and large grew their own food, and the survival and prosperity of the family or clan depended on having a good harvest. If wild animals ate the crops, people trampled them, or enemy armies ate the grain and fruit, it wasn't just a financial loss; starvation was a real possibility. It wasn't like today when you could simply buy every kind of food product at your local supermarket. So, crops were watched over day and night to ensure that they were safely brought to harvest. The watchmen would stand in watchtowers that were built of stone.

A second type of watchman was the guard who stood on the walls of the city. Their responsibility was to watch for enemies and to cry out an alarm if danger approached. Cities in those times were walled to protect the inhabitants from a variety of dangers including marauders, thieves, and enemy forces. Entry was limited to gates, which were carefully observed and guarded. Openings in the gates allowed for weapons to be unleashed against intruders before they could fully enter the city.

Armed watchmen (guards) would pace the walls and watch alertly for anyone who was out of place or appeared suspicious. If they perceived danger, they would call out the alarm, so the men of the city could protect their families. It was especially important to stay awake in the night hours and ensure the safety of the community. Today in Israel, there is still the need for watchmen. Although most of the cities are not walled, many have security fences around the perimeter and guards who monitor everyone who comes and goes.

Ancient watchmen watched over agriculture for families to survive, today, we must watch for tactics and strategies that lower the survival possibilities of families at large. Examples of attacking families: lack of education, glass ceilings of poverty, spiritual and moral decay.

Oversight of City Walls Covering Regions and Territory — Entry was limited to gates, which were carefully observed and guarded. Openings in the gates allowed for weapons to be unleashed against intruders before they could fully enter the city.

Watchmen would stand on a gate, wall, Tower, hill — places of portals; anywhere there is a chance for something to come in or go out. A watcher would take their post. As watchers, we must ask ourselves in relationships, "What are you watching in prayer?" As we watch and pray, we engage in tactics that help us see these are the dimensions of sight.

Dimensions of Sight

Philippians 1:9-10 (AMP):

And this I pray, that your love may abound more and more [displaying itself in greater depth] in real knowledge and in practical insight, 10 so that you may learn to recognize and treasure what is excellent [identifying the best, and distinguishing moral differences], and that you may be pure and blameless until the day of Christ [actually living lives that lead others away from sin]

Sight — the faculty or power of seeing.

Insight — the capacity to gain an accurate and deep intuitive understanding of a person or thing.

Foresight — the ability to predict or the action of predicting what will happen or be needed in the future.

Hindsight — understanding of a situation or event only after it has happened or developed.

These dimensions of sight allow you as the watchman to man the entrances for this city, your house, even your heart. Think about what things can come into your house, family. Who prays for those things? Whose responsibility is it? Whomever responsibility it is cannot afford to get tired, nor nod off. You as the watchman can't afford to be spiritually asleep. Your spirit is willing, but flesh is weak, therefore you must be vigilant and sober at all times.

Functions of the Watchman

SEE, HEAR, and SPEAK

See Vision

Hear and receive prayer

Speak and release prophecy

What are the functions (responsibilities) of the Watchmen:

1.

2.

3.

Key Term: Spiritual Warfare

Explain, using your own terms, the origins of spiritual warfare. Analyze the meaning of this term, its existence, and in what contexts it continues to exist today.

a.

4 Categories of Spiritual Warfare

List and describe

1.

2.

3.

4.

Spiritual Warfare

Fill in the blank.

One of the major weapons of warfare is _____.

    a.

As Watchmen, we don't fight without purpose. Spiritual warfare does come with rewards.

The most premiere reward for fighting is _____.

    b.

Long answer.

Watchmen are defined by having a different perspective. How and in what ways are Watchmen expected to set themselves apart and pursue manifestation of God's will?

    c.

How does the adversary operate?

    d.

Limitations of Warfare

    Long answer.

Though the kingdom of darkness exists, there is a scope of limitations that prevail against it. How is Satan's sphere of influence limited by those who walk with the Light?

     a.

How do Christians operate outside of the world system?

     b.

Prayer

With gratitude and humility, I approach the throne of grace boldly as You have invited me to do. Father, I decree and declare that as the Lord's watchman, I am anointed to receive and interpret the Word of the Lord, convey communication to my era and generation. I thank You for pouring out Your spirit on me in a new, prophetic, and apostolic way that will birth revival, restoration, and regeneration. Lord, I rejoice that when I pray, because You have anointed, appointed, and affirmed me, you respond and answer! I thank You for the seer's anointing; I am not blind spiritually nor naturally — I declare, I see heaven coming into every earthly concern, matter, and situation NOW — in the name of Jesus, Amen!

Reflect and write what the Lord is sharing with you during your time of prayer.

_____

_____

_____

_____

_____

_____

_____

_____

_____

_____

_____

_____

_____

_____

_____

_____

_____

_____

_____

_____

_____

_____

_____

_____

_____

NOTES

Prayer

Oh Lord, I declare Revelation 4:11 (ESV), "Worthy are you, our Lord and God, to receive glory and honor and power, for you created all things, and by your will they existed and were created." You are worthy because you did not create this world and then leave us. Lord, You created us and then promised to be with us and never leave us nor forsake us. For the promises You have made, thank You; I know you to be faithful to all you have spoken. Lord, help me to be the salt of the earth and light in an unbelieving world. I take hold of the assignment and task to stand for righteousness, uphold truth and to be an agent of change in this dark world. I say yes to praying, watching and fasting for supernatural, divine intervention, praying, "Your kingdom come, Your will be done, on earth as it is in heaven" [Matthew 6:10 (NIV)], in Jesus' name, Amen!

Reflect and write what the Lord is sharing with you during your time of prayer.

_____

_____

_____

_____

_____

_____

_____

_____

_____

_____

_____

_____

_____

_____

_____

_____

_____

_____

_____

_____

_____

_____

_____

_____

NOTES

Responsibilities of a Watchman

The responsibilities of the watchman include,

Know the condition of your heart at all times.

Be able to hear clearly

Know who/what you're called to watch over.

Be able to see precisely; even into the future (prophetic fore sight)

Know why you're watching over

Use effective communication technology and jargon

Called to a lifestyle of holiness (character, spiritual maturity, discipline, seasoned appetite for the Word, intercession) Prayer — An important part of the prophets' task is prayer. Because they know the mind of the Lord, they are in a position to pray effectively. They have a clear picture of what God is doing, so he knows where prayer is needed most. The prophets watch over the word of the Lord and pray it into being. They must not rest until God has fulfilled his word (Isaiah 62:6). Operate in jurisdictional prophetic power in prayer. A key role of the prophet is waiting in the presence of God to receive the word of God. God is sovereign, so we cannot tell him when he should speak. Hearing will always require waiting. Prophetic people experience levels of suffering. Deep dealing at the hand of God will often be needed to prepare the prophet for receiving the word of God. Sometimes we may actually have to experience beforehand, something of what his people will experience Worship. Interpreting seasons and times. They are called to have excellent character.

Watchman's Call of Character

Love for God

Commitment to Holiness

Righteous Zeal

Grasp Divine Truth

Aware of Sin Nature

Desire to Mature Believers

Aware of Sin's Cure

Allegiance to God

Upholds Truth Giving God's Judgment for Sin

Rebuke Wrongdoers

Warn Believers of Danger

Surrendered to Christ

Identity Hide in Christ

Obedient & Submissive

Seeks God-Approved Training

Nurtures/Trains Others

Unique Prophetic Insight

Strong Conviction

Defensive About Christ & Gospel

Protective of Kingdom

Protective/Reveres God

Respects God's Justice

Disregards Worldliness

Refrains from gossip

Has Contempt for Worldliness in the Body of Christ

Reputable reputation

Constant Longing for God's Kingdom to Come in the Earth

Strong Sense of Duty

Strong Need for God's Continuous Fellowship

Knowledge of Scope & Responsibility of Prophetic Office

Relentless Hunger for God's Presence

With these characteristics and traits, watchmen create a prophetic intercession culture.

Prayer

Abba Father, You are such a loving Father and gracious Savior You are. Thank You for the grace to pray and faint not. You have anointed me to intercede on behalf of _____ [name anyone, anything, or anywhere you're being led to intercede for], I do not lose heart nor turn blessed hope loose. I thank You that in this set hour, I pray in the Spirit — through the gift of tongues and the power of travail. Lord, grant me patience to tarry, waiting on You to appear, speak and move as I pray. I call out to the LORD, and You answer me from Your holy mountain [Psalm 3:4]. My soul magnifies the Lord, who takes pleasure in my prosperity [Psalm 35:27]. I decree and declare, my prayers prosper in the Spirit and in prevail in the natural because I pray under the Spirit of the LORD, spirit of wisdom, understanding, counsel, strength, knowledge and in the fear of the Lord. I lay hold to answers, solutions, resolves and heaven's decisions to earthly matters in the name of the Lord Jesus! I call down answers and heaven's intervention, NOW by the Spirit of Might! In the name of Jesus, Amen!

Reflect and write what the Lord is sharing with you during your time of prayer.

_____

_____

_____

_____

_____

_____

_____

_____

_____

_____

_____

_____

_____

_____

NOTES

The Intersection of Intercession & Influence

Influence for the intercessor means, involves movement, it embodies direction. It focuses on the ways God communicates. When assigned to be a watchman, one of the key areas you guard and watch over is the portals of influence. Satan uses the spirit of Jezebel to be the driving force to infect influence.

The Written Word: The logos (the Bible) is a main way God speaks today, but it is not the only way. The logos is God's general Word for everyone. God speaks to us when we read the Bible on nearly every issue that applies to modern living. Jesus, the Bread of Life, taught us to pray, "Give us this day our daily bread" (Mt. 6:11). God has fresh spiritual manna to share with us every day if we'll take the time to read His Word.

Key Principles To Know

• We are all equally loved by God but not all equally anointed by God. Our anointing comes by way of our assignment. Based on our assignment, God gives grace.

• Another word for assignment is responsibility.

• Increased oil = increased responsibility.

• Prophets, prophetic intercessors, apostles MUST be open to responsibility. • Levels of responsibility: health (body, soul [mental and emotional space])

• You must take responsibility for your own trauma. Only when you take responsibility over your trauma will you be able to take authority over your history, and it will begin to work for you. • You cannot work it if you're still asking why — why did it happen? • Complaining is a sign that you're losing the battle of your thoughts. If you have an issue, and you take it to God — leave it with God and trust His outcome. (Romans 8:28)

     • Complaining people often have a poor prayer life. (Philippians 4:7-9)

Traffic Control

     • **<u>Ezekiel 28:5 (KJV)</u>** — *By thy great wisdom and by thy traffic hast thou increased thy riches, and thine heart is lifted   up because of thy riches:*

     • **<u>Ezekiel 28:16 (KJV)</u>** — *By the multitude of thy merchandise they have filled the midst with thee with violence, and thou hast sinned: therefore I will cast thee as profane out of the mountain of God: and I will destroy thee, O covering   cherub, from the midst of the stones of fire.*

The traffic is not on a highway, but it's in your mind/the intake and output of your soul.

Your mental and emotional space is the edge of the spiritual world because it is the gateway of expression. If we fail to manage our mental and emotional gate, we will always misinterpret what we see and hear in the spiritual world.

How God Communicates

God communicated through and to all dimensions of man: body, mind and soul. No part of us is cut off from divine communication. When God desires to manifest or demonstrate in the Earth, He does it through you. He has to first drop it as a thought, feeling; it has to permeate, swell and grow and God will begin to speak. When God speaks, He uses several different avenues; it's not always audible. God can speak through your emotions and what He says will often times be communicated through a feeling and not a word. How can you trust the feeling when your soul is broken? Manage the gate of expression which is your soul. You're only as valuable as your soul is healthy. The enemy works overtime making the saints insane! Don't be so concerned with being deep hearing God that you miss the voice of your own soul: I'm going to commit suicide, I'm depressed, I'm tired, etc. You must become familiar with your own grace, anointing and even voice.

Soul Health

Much like the growth of a tree, the soul's evolution depends on the health of the elements available to it. In the case of the soul's evolution, the humanly elements of life are the basis for unimpeded growth. The branches of the tree represent 10 primary areas of the human condition which must be in balance for the soul's most optimal growth and evolution. These include Physical, Psychological, Interpersonal, Social, Financial, Intellectual, Environmental, Sexual, Spiritual, and Recreational branches of health. These branches bridge the gap between the human condition and the soul. The entirety of the tree represents the interplay between these two aspects of our existence and illustrates the impact on the rest of our human condition when one or more branches are not healthy. The model emphasizes that when one branch is broken it is impossible for the rest of the tree to remain unaffected. Even one unhealthy branch can have a traumatic impact on the soul's overall health.

Ways God Communicates: Holy Spirit

The Holy Spirit should be the central and main foundation every time God speaks, be it when we are reading the word, or through a person or a circumstance. He acts as our inner witness to reveal and confirm deep things to us. Through discernment (a solid knowing, sensing or conviction), a tug in your heart or a gut feeling, we would recognize the Holy Spirit.

Ways God Communicates: Theophany

• Physical manifestation of the glory of God or God Himself

• A *theophany* is an appearance of God. More precisely, it is a visible display to human beings that expresses the presence and character of God. Examples include the thunderous display at the top of Mount Sinai (Ex. 19); the burning bush (Ex. 3); appearances to Abraham (Gen. 15:1; 17:1; 18:1), Isaac (Gen. 26:2), and Jacob (Gen. 28:13); the cloud of fire in the wilderness (Ex. 14:19; 40:34; Numbers. 9:15-23); Micaiah's vision (1 Kings 22:19-22); Isaiah's vision (Isa. 6); Ezekiel's vision (Ezekiel. 1); and John's vision of God on his throne (Rev. 4-5).

   • Spirit world communicates through thoughts (sphere of your mind), feelings, emotions, memory (events → nostalgia)

   • Nostalgia — gateway of time; example: music can trigger your memory that creates a portal for you to step back into your past. Nostalgia — a sentimental longing or wistful affection for the past, typically for a period or place with happy personal associations.

   • Demons can hide behind memories that only manifest when triggered.

Ways God Communicates: Paths in Prayer

• Prayer is a pathway into the supernatural and spiritual realm.

• Once you start to pray and focus on God to lead you, He starts to give you what to actually pray about — be it in your understanding or in the Spirit.

• Example: You might go into prayer for your family, and you suddenly don't know why you are praying about your job and specifically not to be fired.

• In a case like this, it may not make sense to you, but Holy Spirit guides us in the best way to pray and what to pray about. This could translate to "be careful at your job", "to take your job more seriously" or "to beware of any surprises that may come from work."

Ways God Communicates: Verbal

• Internal/Inaudible: primary mode of communication —"still small voice of God"

• External/Audible: God emphasizing a word, message, phrase, term in the voice of another person (when you hear what they didn't say — rhema)

Ways God Communicates: Audible Voice

God has and still can speak audibly.

• Adam and Eve heard God's voice in the Garden of Eden (Gen. 3:8).

• God spoke audibly to Moses from the burning bush (Ex. 3:4-6) and to all Israel from Mount Sinai (Ex. 20:1-22).

• In the New Testament, the Father endorsed Jesus at His baptism and His transfiguration with a literal voice. Saul and his posse saw Christ in a blinding light and heard His voice (Ac. 9:3-7).

Ways God Communicates: Verbal

• There are two legal voices in your spirit:

• Conscience — an inner feeling or voice viewed as acting as a guide to the rightness or wrongness of one's behavior. God hard-wired us with an inner awareness of what is right and wrong with an inclination to do right.

• Still Small Voice — (**1 Kings 19:12**) gentle stillness or peace; in Hebrew means, a whisper [In the stillness of God's presence, God will give you clarity) Ways God Communicates: Still Small Voice

• Elijah was camping in a cave on Mount Sinai when God manifested Himself. Elijah saw a powerful wind, a mighty earthquake and a fierce fire, but God wasn't in any of them. Instead, God spoke to him in a "still small voice," also translated "a gentle whisper" (**1 Kings. 19:9-12**).

• God often speaks to us by the inner witness of the Holy Spirit to our spirit (**Romans 8:14-16**).

Ways God Communicates: Dreams and Visions

"I will pour out of My Spirit on all flesh. . . your young men shall see visions, your old men shall dream dreams" (**Acts 2:17***)*.

• A **vision** is an inspired appearance (something you see literally with your eyes or in your mind or spirit); how the Lord uses the creativity of your imagination to relay a message to you; these require additional reflection and prayer interpretation (some interpretations can take years to make sense)

• A **dream** is something seen in your sleep or something you imagine doing—a goal or an aspiration. God can insert images and ideas into our minds whether we are conscious or not.

• **Encounters** — intentional experiences that reveal God's character and develops you. You grow faith grows, wisdom rises from encounters.; repeated instances.

Ways God Communicates: Repeated Instances

When similar things re-occur over a space of time, it might just be God calling your attention to something. An example can be as simple as your eye twitching anytime you are about to get angry. It might just be God saying "it's not worth it." I want you to understand that when you have a close-knit relationship with God, he talks to you every time and very easily. He is not shy around you, and He doesn't keep mute; you are His child. He'll talk, he'll warn you, he'll correct you, he'll make you laugh. There are no coincidences. Pay attention and try to hear what God is saying to you always.

Ways God Communicates: Intellectual Reasoning

• God works with the knowledge you know.

• God can give you supernatural wisdom and insight but for a need in a moment, but God will always use you at the level of your intellectual reasoning; academia

• Cognitive reasoning, connecting pieces of a puzzle

• Imagination — is the ability to produce and simulate novel objects, peoples and ideas in the mind without any immediate input of the senses. God can also work through imagery. Example: The knee problem = lack of intercession.

Ways God Communicates: Tongues & Interpretation

1 Corinthians 14:27 (ESV) — *If any speak in a tongue, let there be only two or at most three, and each in turn, and let someone interpret.*

Ways God Communicates: Signs

• Gideon put a fleece out sincerely seeking confirmation of God's will and was obliged (Judges 6:36-40). We serve a supernatural God of signs and wonders.

Ways God Communicates: People

"If anyone speaks, let him speak as the oracles of God" (**1 Peter 4:11**).

• An "oracle" is an "utterance, a spokesman or mouthpiece." God speaks through preachers and teachers, but He can also speak through our spouse, kids, friends and even enemies.

• God uses human channels to speak words of prophecy, tongues and interpretation and words of wisdom and knowledge (**1 Cor. 12:8-10**).

• God also expresses Himself through human vessels to distribute His message in anointed sermons, songs and writings.

Ways God Communicates: Media

• God also utilizes the media to disseminate His truth via satellite TV, radio, internet, websites, social media, books, podcasts, movies and music.

Ways God Communicates: Creation/Nature

• Through Creation and Nature: Psalms 19:1 proclaims, "The heavens declare the glory of God; and the firmament shows His handiwork." The vastness of space and the complexity of nature testify to God's intelligent design.

Prayer

Lord, I approach Your throne with thanksgiving for all that You have done for me! My heart flows with waters of appreciation, my hands are lifted in praise, my mouth utters Your worth! According to Acts 1:8, I have been filled with power. Because I have been filled with heavenly power and authority, my steps are ordered by the Lord, You have filled my mouth with good things and the blessing of the Lord is on all I do and put my hands to. Lord, have mercy on mankind. I intercede for the body of Christ and ask that Your sufficient grace will be extended to us anew. Holy Spirit, equip us to be Your intercessors that can be trusted with influence. Help us to be stewards of the influence You have graced us with; may we honor, represent, and reflect You in all that we do. I owe You [God] my influence! Thank You for the capacity and power to have holy effects on people, places, regions, organizations, entities, and the world — all for Your glory! Get the glory, take the honor, it's all Yours! In the name of Jesus, Amen!

Reflect and write what the Lord is sharing with you during your time of prayer.

_____

_____

_____

_____

_____

_____

_____

_____

_____

_____

_____

_____

_____

_____

_____

_____

_____

_____

_____

_____

_____

_____

_____

_____

NOTES

Covering Families

We've talked about ancient practices that are still very applicable and can be used today. Ancient watchmen watched over agriculture for families to survive, today, we must watch for tactics and strategies that lower the survival possibilities of families at large. Examples of attacking families: lack of education, glass ceilings of poverty, spiritual and moral decay.

Oversight of City Walls Covering Regions and Territory — Entry was limited to gates, which were carefully observed and guarded. Openings in the gates allowed for weapons to be unleashed against intruders before they could fully enter the city.

Prayer

Merciful Savior, I thank You that 'family' is Your design. I pray according to Joshua 24:15, my family serves only the LORD. I intercede and cover my family in the Word of God. Your Word says, You are always watching over us. You are the mighty warrior who saves — I ask Lord that You would protect my family under Your mighty wings of protection according to Psalm 91. I declare that no evil will befall our dwelling places [Psalm 91:10]. My entire family lives under the Shadow of the Almighty, being hidden from calamity, dangers, evil and trouble. I intercede on behalf of my unsaved loved ones and call them by faith into the ark of safety — declaring their time of salvation has come! Thank You for granting my bloodline Your perfect peace that surpasses all understanding. My family is a unit of love, peace, joy, and laughter! We give no room to the spirit of confusion, hatred, jealousy, or discord in the name of Jesus. Thank You Holy Ghost that my family is full of compassion for You and towards one another. We speak gentle, kind words to each other. We are a family of harmony. My family is wise, healthy, and wealthy. I break every generational curse with the blood of Jesus according to Galatians 3:19. Therefore I thank You that just as your presence was with the family of Obed-Edom in 1 Chronicles 13:14, so is Your presence with my family. I thank You, Lord, for blessing my family, every household in my bloodline and everything we have. Wealth and riches are in the house of the righteous! The marriages in my family are blessed, our children are blessed, our homes are blessed — and generations to come will tell of Your goodness and serve You! In Jesus' name, Amen!

*Call your family name[s] out before the Lord when you pray!

Reflect and write what the Lord is sharing with you during your time of prayer.

_____

_____

_____

_____

_____

_____

_____

_____

_____

_____

_____

_____

_____

_____

_____

_____

_____

_____

_____

_____

_____

_____

NOTES

Covering Churches

Prayer

Father, on the authority of Your Word, I cover in prayer, stand in the gap for _____ [name the church or ministry in which you're interceding for]. I decree and declare that You have built this church/ministry and the gates of hell will not prevail against it. I speak by faith, this church is the church in which you designed it to be — fruitful, populous, supernatural, Christ-centered and Holy Spirit empowered! Thank You, Lord my church does not lack the anointing, not void of Your glory and presence, nor does it lack anything necessary to be effective in the earth. I thank You that the Word of God is taught at my church, supplying my pastor _____ [mention his/her name] with rhema knowledge, teaching and preaching power accompanied with signs and wonders as it was with the apostles. I call by faith my church is a place where sinners are saved, saints are delivered, gifts are groomed, and we serve mankind. Lord, I pray that you will stir the hearts of the believers to all be intercessors; may the embers for prayer in our hearts never burn out. Bless all leaders and partners a part of this kingdom mandate. I pray Lord, disciples are birthed in this place, in the name of Jesus. People come from the north, south, east, and west because my church bears witness to miracles, signs, and wonders — consistently. I humbly ask that You release Your revival winds, prophetic Word, and miraculous power in a new way as Your Word references in Isaiah 43:19. I speak now against the adversary and command every attack, plot, and plan of hell against this church to be held hostage by God's mighty power! Build this house Lord, may the vision pros-per, may the people thrive, through Christ our Lord, Amen!

Reflect and write what the Lord is sharing with you during your time of prayer.

_____
_____
_____
_____
_____
_____
_____
_____
_____
_____
_____
_____
_____
_____
_____
_____
_____
_____
_____
_____
_____
_____
_____

NOTES

Covering Relationships

Prayer

Dear Heavenly Father, it has been Your Will that man not be alone. I thank You, Lord that it is Your will that I prosper in every area of my life, including my relationships. Holy Spirit, because you have loved me was extended to me, grace, love, mercy, and grace is what I extend to all whom I connect with. I confess by faith that my connections, friendships, and relationships are godly. If anyone that I am connected to falls down, I thank You for equipping me with the strength, skill and sensitivity to help the other up. Lord, I pray that none of my relationships are un-equally yoked, in the name of Jesus but my relationships are edifying, empowering, and encouraging. I come against every distracting connection, connections sent from the enemy to distract and destroy — we cancel your influence and attraction now in the name of Jesus. I decree that I walk with those whom I agree with in the Spirit. I thank You, Lord, for pure, prosperous connections and the godly counsel that surrounds me in the name of Jesus. I commit to guarding my heart with all diligence, for from it flows the issues of life [Proverbs 4:23]. I pray that I walk with wise people, and I shall become wise. Holy Spirit, partner me with individuals that are like iron so that I might be sharpened! I pray Lord that I will gain relationships with men and women of influence, integrity, and intellect spiritually and naturally. I pray Father that I always show myself friendly for I know not when I shall be entertaining an angel [Hebrews 13:2]. It is so and done in Jesus' name, Amen.

Reflect and write what the Lord is sharing with you during your time of prayer.

_____

_____

_____

_____

_____

_____

_____

_____

_____

_____

_____

_____

_____

_____

_____

_____

_____

_____

_____

_____

_____

_____

_____

NOTES

Eight Watches of Prayer

"But we prayed to our God and guarded the city day and night to protect ourselves." **Nehemiah 4: 9 (NLT)**

Scriptures speak of "watches," which covers different spans of time throughout any given day. The biblical term for watch is "shamar" meaning to see, to keep, guard, keep watch and ward, protect, wait for, and to retain. Everyone has a prayer "shamar" watch, even though they may not be aware of it. This is why we may find ourselves compelled to pray or sense a mood shift at specific times during the morning, midday or evening. During those times the Holy Spirit is in need of "you" to partner with Him and stand in the gap and strategically intercede for what He impresses upon your spirit. You are needed to disrupt and dismantle the diabolical plans of the enemy and to assist in opening up the gates and portals for the great things of God to legally take place in the earth.

These eight watches are for the purpose of saturating the earth and all creation with God's glory. We need the Holy Spirit and God's Angels to help us and the Holy Spirit and God's Angels need us to arise early on our watches to decree and strategically cover our earthly basis from our Heavenly Headquarters. If you have ever been awakened during the night or are wondering why you are being led to pray at specific times, it is almost certainly because God wants you to pray or intercede for someone or something. Romans 8:14, tells us, "For those who are led by the Spirit of God are the children of God." At times, we willingly and unwillingly fail to obey the voice and leading of Holy Spirit. Don't resist the urge to pray or give in to the temptation to draw back in prayer.

Nothing happens in the earth and to creation until words are spoken. It is our responsibility as Ambassadors for Christ to uphold the highest standards of righteousness from the Kingdom of God on our watches. We are God's personal representatives in the earth to pray and decree His Word over ourselves, families and marriages in the earth, our cities, governments, nations and the atmosphere.

Actively flowing with the Holy Spirit and staying in tune with others on our watches shifts the atmosphere and situations around us. Now that we are up on our watch, now what? The whole creation waits breathless with anticipation for the revelation of God's sons and daughters.

Prayer

"I will take my stand at my watch post and station myself on the tower and look out to see what he will say to me, and what I will answer concerning my complaint."

Habakkuk 2:1 (ESV)

Holy Spirit, I take hold of the invitation to come boldly before the throne of grace, to receive mercy and divine aid in times of need [Hebrews 4:16]. Lord, thank You for allowing me access to the chambers of Your glory. Holy Spirit, reveal to me my ordained hour of intercession. Unclose to me the time of day or night you are calling me to be a watchman on the wall. During my watch hour, may deep calleth unto deep [Psalm 42:7], incline Your ear to Your servant! I pray in alignment to Psalm 103:20, "Bless the Lord, O you his angels, you mighty ones who do His Word, obeying the voice of His Word!" I release the angels of the Most High God to go swiftly to every matter, place, person, entity and industry I mention in prayer in the mighty name of Jesus! Lord, help me to stand my watch — praying, travailing, tarrying — calling on the name of the Lord, being confident that You hear me when I call! In the name that changes everything, Jesus, Amen!

Reflect and write what the Lord is sharing with you during your time of prayer.

_____

_____

_____

_____

_____

_____

_____

_____

_____

_____

_____

_____

_____

_____

_____

_____

_____

_____

_____

_____

_____

_____

_____

NOTES

Watch One (The Evening Watch: 6pm-9pm)

When evening came, the disciples came to Him and said, "This is an isolated place and the hour is already late; send the crowds away so that they may go into the villages and buy food for themselves." — **Matthew 14:15**

Watch One is a time span of meditation, quiet reflection and renewal with the Holy Spirit. Minds are transformed and decisions are made during this time span. Decrees, strategic prayers and judgments with the Holy Spirit's leading are pronounced upon those in the occult before they begin their active sorcery starting at the midnight watch. God strengthens His people during this watch and reveals His Fatherhood and renewing His covenant with them.

Whatever happens during the day is largely determined by what is done during the night watches. The evening time span is the beginning of all the watches. Intercessors can strategically command the enemies of God and stand in the gap and prevent the kingdom of darkness from releasing curses in and on their new days and humanity by dismantling the high places that the enemy has set up over regions.

Scriptures that are targeted on this time span:
> Genesis 9:15-16
> Exodus 2:24
> Leviticus 26:42-45
> Psalm 16
> Psalm 32
> Psalm 34

Psalm 37

Psalm 105:8

Psalm 119:105-111

Jeremiah 15:16

Romans 8:14-15

Galatians3:26-2

Hebrews 8:10-12

<u>Decrees and Strategic Prayers Points:</u>

- Enter His gates with a song of thanksgiving and His courts with praise. Be thankful to Him, bless and praise His name.

- Pray in the Holy Spirit "tongues"

- Pray in alignment with what the Holy Spirit is revealing to you at the moment on this watch

- Pray for clarity regarding the upcoming new day and His call upon your life

- Decree that you are God's child and His words are what sustain you in every situation

Prayer

O Lord, I delight in Your law, meditating on it day and night! Father, as I come into the first watch of prayer, I call my attention to horn in solely on Your goodness, mercy, and faithfulness You daily demonstrate to me. Lord, I lay hold to having the mind of Christ and confess that Jesus is LORD over my mind, body, and soul. I call forth a renewed mind in the name of Jesus as I release all my cares, burdens, stressors, pressure, and concerns from the day. I pray Father that all decisions made today bring glory to Your name. Thank You for washing me with the water of Your Word. I declare truth over every concern and matter; I lay it all at Your feet. I cast my cares upon the Lord, knowing You care for me. I declare that my mind is stayed on You, therefore peace is my portion. I call a halt to self-sabotaging thoughts, low thinking, fatigue faith, and vain imaginations. My mind belongs to God; I do not have brain fog, but rather clear thinking, and I am in tune with the voice of the Good Shepherd. I command every demonic force, attack and maneuver that had been released against me this day to not be null and void. I bring down every stronghold that is exalting itself against the knowledge of God. I decree that God is very God and His reign is forever, and JESUS is Lord! In Jesus' name, Amen.

Reflect and write what the Lord is sharing with you during your time of prayer.

NOTES

Watch Two (The Night Watch: 9pm-Midnight)

I get up in the middle of the night to thank you; your decisions are so right, so true — I can't wait till morning! —

Psalm 119:62

This is a prime time for praise and worship before the new day enters. It was at the midnight hour that God struck down the first-born of Egypt, which resulted in His people being released from captivity and set free to worship Him. This watch is a time when God deals with the enemies that are trying to keep us from entering into His perfect plan for our lives. Watch Two is a high time span to arise and permeate the spiritual atmosphere of darkness before those in the occult get prepared to release diabolical assignments and sabotage families, cities and nations in the universe. Midnight is symbolic of intense darkness, but God is the light that dispels darkness and releases strategies during this time to defeat our enemies as we decree and pray strategically as the Holy Spirit leads us. We are set free and released to praise and worship God and offer up thanksgiving to Him as we enter and experience His perfect will for our lives on this time span.

Scriptures that are targeted on this time span:

Psalm 35

Psalm 59

Psalm 68

Psalm 91

Psalm 119:62

Psalm 148

2 Corinthians 10:3-5

Ephesians 6:10-18

Decrees and Strategic Prayers Points:

- Enter His gates with a song of thanksgiving and His courts with praise. Be thankful to Him, bless and praise His name.
- Pray in the Holy Spirit "tongues"
- Pray for God's protection over your life, families, cities, governments and nations
- Pray for freedom of those captured by the enemy's traps
- Declare that God will arise and scatter His enemies and all curses are null and void
- Praise and worship exalting God and commanding all creation to praise Him.

Has the Holy Spirit led you to this watch? Creation waits in eager expectation for you to be revealed!

Prayer

Father, in the name of Jesus, I thank You because You are good, and Your mercy endures forever! Lord, in this second watch of prayer, I intercede, stand in the gap for my family _____[mention every last name attached to your family line], I pray for _____[mention your city], our government and all nations. Lord, I pray against all forms of evil concerning my life, my family, my region, government, and international affairs. Lord, I pray according to Psalm 91:3, "Surely He will deliver you from the snare of the enemy." I pray now, every snare be broken in Jesus' name, and I thank You for breakthrough, deliverance, and divine rescues in Jesus' name! But you, LORD, are a shield around me, my glory, the One who lifts my head high! Lift my head high above my enemies, lift my head high above the affairs of this life, the demands of my energy and attention. Lord, lift my knowledge above those of the kingdom of darkness, lift my eyes above them that do evil, lift my intellect and understanding above mediocrity, in the name of Jesus! I pray that God arise and His enemies be scattered now, in the name of the Lord Jesus! Father, I bless You for Your faithfulness to provide victory and for disarming the powers and authorities and for shaming them publicly by Your victory over them on the cross according to Colossians 2:15. In the name of Christ, our Lord, Amen!

Reflect and write what the Lord is sharing with you during your time of prayer.

_____

_____

_____

_____

_____

_____

_____

_____

_____

_____

_____

_____

_____

_____

_____

_____

_____

NOTES

Watch Three (Midnight-3am)

"Behold, I give you the authority to trample on serpents and scorpions, and over all the power of the enemy, and nothing shall by any means hurt you."— **Luke 10:19**

This is a period of much spiritual activity. This watch hour will strengthen your faith. It is the same time that Peter denied Christ three times. (Matthew 26: 34, 74; Mark 14:30; Luke 22:34; John 13:38). Watch Three is a high time span to strengthen your faith and command the morning in the darkest part of the night watch. An outpouring of God's fresh anointing and grace is released to overcome limitations. High praises, worship, decrees and strategic prayers are boldly released and declared to overrule the pronouncements of sorcerers. The enemy works the hardest during this time span as most people are vulnerable due to the deep rem sleep level and aren't alert to prevent his tactics. During this witching hour, intercessors arise spiritually clothed with the armor of the Lord as they enter into the high places of the heavenly realms and release warfare prayers for the release of prisoners and those who have been tempted by the enemy's suggestions and lies.

The Witching Hour

This watch is the darkest and most demonic part of the night, especially at midnight. Witches, warlocks, and satanists have fun and start their incantations during this part of the night. The devil operates at this time because this is the time that men are in a deep sleep and there are not as many people praying to oppose him (1 Kings

3:20). This watch calls for seasoned intercessors. You must not be afraid of witchcraft during this watch. The Lord has given us dominion and authority over all things. This watch is geared for those who already know how to use their spiritual armor and war against the enemy. This is the time to pray against satanic attacks on your life, family members, marriages, churches and communities. We are most vulnerable to the devil's attacks because at this time we are asleep. Declare Psalm 91:5-6 for Divine protection for yourself, family, church, city and nation.

Time to set your day before it begins. This is a powerful watch to be on when commanding the morning and setting things in place before the devil and his demons have a chance to ruin it. Plane crashes, car crashes, deaths, job loss, and many other acts of the devil can be stopped during this watch when intercessors obey the voice of the Lord and saturate this time with powerful, Spirit-led prayers. This is the time for spiritual warfare.

This is the time to awake out of sleep and confront every storm of destruction and distraction that is robbing you of God's blessings and provisions on your life. Also, it is the time to speak peace and calm into every situation of turbulence and confusion. **Time to strengthen yourself spiritually and seek direction.**

Be vigilant during this time and watch for God's revelation for breakthrough and for His plans and purposes for your life and territory.

Time to pray for release from every prison. The Apostle Paul and Silas were released from prison during this time (Acts 16:25). In addition, God released the people of Israel from Egypt at this time (Exodus 12:31). According to Judges16:3-4, Samson escaped from

Gaza at midnight by pulling up the gates of the city and carrying them out with him.

Time to make your case in prayer.

This is the period to pray for God's provision to be released (Luke 11:5-13; Acts 16:3). It is also time for miracles and for applying the Blood of Jesus.

Dreams flow during this hour.

Often, we are awakened during this time with dreams God has given to us. God uses dreams and visions to bring instruction and counsel to us as we sleep. He also reveals areas where we need to concentrate our prayers and intercession. "In a dream, in a vision of the night, when deep sleep falls upon men, while slumbering on their beds, then He opens the ears of men, and seals their instructions." (**Job 33:15**).

The devil can also attack you in dreams (nightmares), so always pray before you go to sleep and ask God to keep you from the enemy's devices. Most dreams and nightmares occur during this time span. Prayers lifted up and asking the Holy Spirit and ministering Angels to keep yourself and others from the enemy's schemes is crucial before going to sleep. You are God's beloved, and He promised that you would be kept safe and go to bed without fear and sleep soundly. Spirit-led decrees and strategic prayers against satanic attacks on your life, family members, marriages, churches, cities, communities, governments and nations are cancelled on this time span.

Scriptures that are targeted during this time span :

Psalm 4:8

Psalm 37: 4

Psalm 91

Job 33:15

Isaiah 54:17

Philippians 4:19 are targeted on this time span.

Watch Three Decrees and Strategic Prayers Points:

- Pray for angelic intervention and protection from satanic attacks for your life, family members, marriages, churches, cities, communities, governments and nations

- Pray for an outpouring of God's fresh anointing and grace to overcome limitations

- Pray that all of the enemy's plans fail and no weapons that were formed against your life, family members, marriages, churches, cities, communities, governments and nations will prosper

- Decree that you are anointed and have been given by God dominion, authority and power to tread upon all the power of the enemy, and you are strong in the Lord and in the power of His might.

- High praises and worship during this time span to establish God as the only King, Lord, and Exalted One with all power and might.

Prayer

O Lord, how great is Your name in all the earth! I bow before You in reverence to Your holy name — Who is faithful and true. There is no failure in You. There is no deceit in Your character or reputation. I thank You now for exalting my horn like that of the wild ox; you have poured over me fresh oil — hallelujah [Psalm 92:10]! You prepare tables before me in the presence of mine enemies, you anointed my head with oil and my cup runs over, Lord [Psalm 23:5]! Oh, my soul blesses Your name! You have made me glad Father! Lord, I thank You for a fresh anointing and grace to overcome limitations during this watch of prayer [12am — 3am]. I bless you Lord those restrictions, restraints, constraints, walls, hindrances are being brought down now in the name of Jesus! I command every wall that has been erected to hinder kingdom purposes to crumble now in Jesus' name! We destroy glass ceilings and break curses now in the name of the Lord Jesus! I pray in Jesus' name, that God is able NOW to do exceedingly, abundantly above all that we ask or think, according to the power that worketh in us [Ephesians 3:20]. Lord, as I go up into the heavenly realms of prayer, into warfare, I pray for the release of prisoners and those who have been tempted by the enemy's suggestions and lies. Strengthen me where I am weak Holy Spirit. Grant Your servant direction and one more time, strength to the inner man. In Jesus' name, Amen.

Reflect and write what the Lord is sharing with you during your time of prayer.

_____

_____

_____

_____

_____

_____

_____

_____

_____

_____

_____

_____

_____

_____

_____

_____

_____

_____

_____

_____

_____

_____

NOTES

Watch Four (3am-6am)

"You will also decide and decree a thing, and it will be established for you; And the light [of God's favor] will shine upon your ways."

Job 22:28

Watch Four is another spiritually high time span for the Angelic host to divinely intervene and minister on the behalf of intercessors that have commanded them to cancel the pronouncements of witches and sorcerers. During this time span new territories are gained and established as God releases the dew of heaven, prosperity and favor. All of the enemy's plans for accidents, premature deaths, thefts, job losses and demonic activity are terminated as intercessors permeate the atmosphere with powerful prophetic Spirit-led decrees and strategic prayers.

Scriptures that are targeted on this time span:
Exodus 12
Exodus 14
Deuteronomy 28:7
Psalm 19:2
Psalm 112
Psalm 121:6
Proverbs 16:3
Job 22:27-28
Isaiah 54:17
Matthew 24:43

John 10:10

Acts 10:38

1 Corinthians 15:58

Decrees and Strategic Prayers Points:

- Enter His gates with a song of thanksgiving and His courts with praise. Be thankful to Him, bless and praise His name.
- Pray in the Holy Spirit "tongues"
- Pray that God's will be done in earth as it is already established in heaven
- Pray that everything that has died in your life and the Body of Christ, in terms of potentials, are released and all losses restored
- Pray the prayer of Jabez
- Decree that God's plans will succeed in every area of your life and everything that your hands touch prospers

Prayer

Elohim, the God who creates — oh, how I praise Your righteous acts! Consistent in all Your ways. You are ever abiding with us and watching over Your Word to perform it. Lord, I thank You that the power of life and death is in my tongue. I thank You that I can decree a thing, and it shall be established. Lord, I thank You that when I speak Your Word, it does what it was sent to do, not returning void or bankrupt [Isaiah 55:11]. Your Word never returns without having fulfilled its purpose! You have sent forth Your Word and healed us, delivering us from the door of death [Psalm 107:20]. This is the hour of Your Word! Angels are being dispatched now to perform the Word of the Lord! Your eyes are upon the righteous, and Your ears attend to their prayers! Holy Spirit, I pray for angelic backup for prayers prayed in this watch. I pray Lord in the Spirit at this time — I claim new territories now in Jesus' name, release the dew of heaven, prosperity and favor upon the land!

I cancel the devil's destructive plans and acts of devastation against God's people — accidents, premature deaths, thefts, job losses, demonic activity be terminated now in the name of Jesus! Holy Spirit, plead on my behalf, make intercession through the moaning and groanings of the Spirit. O Holy Spirit, put Your word down in me! Put fresh fire in my belly. Cause rivers of living water to flow out of me, in the name of Jesus! It is Christ who causes us to always triumph, Hallelujah! In Jesus' name, Amen.

Reflect and write what the Lord is sharing with you during your time of prayer.

_____
_____
_____
_____
_____
_____
_____
_____
_____
_____
_____
_____
_____
_____
_____
_____
_____
_____
_____
_____
_____
_____
_____

NOTES

Watch Five (6am-9am)

But for you who fear My name with awe-filled reverence the sun of righteousness will rise with healing in its wings. And you will go forward and leap joyfully like calves released from the stall.

<u>Malachi 4:2</u>

Watch Five is a time span of the beginning of the day watches, the night intercessors or watchmen's shifts are completed and there's a changing of the guards to take their position on the wall. A time of renewal for the soul and strengthening the spirit and body for the service of the Holy Spirit. The sun of righteousness will dawn on those who honor God's name, healing radiating from its wings. Bursting energies manifested and triumphant voices of victory over the enemy are heightened during this time span. Nothing but ashes are under the feet of intercessors that have treaded upon the wicked plans and assignments of the enemy from the previous watches. The enemy is a defeated foe and reminded of his place and position of defeat.

On this watch prophetic decrees and strategic prayers and utterances are released for forgiveness, divine healing for those who have been bound by the spirit of infirmity, the spirit of bondage, and hidden spirits, relationships, finances, government, and the economy are reversed, released and restored from the strongholds of the enemy. This time span is a time of refreshing. Breathe...

Scriptures that are targeted on this time span:

Malachi 4:2

Psalm 2:7-9

Psalm 103:1-12

Psalm 107:20

Proverbs 10:7

Isaiah 54:3-5

Matthew 8:17

Luke 10:19

Acts 1:8

Acts 2:15

Romans 12:1-2

2 Corinthians 10:3-5

Ephesians 4:12

Philippians 4:13

1 Peter 2:24

1 John 1:9

Decrees and Strategic Prayers Points:

● Enter His gates with a song of thanksgiving and His courts with praise. Be thankful to Him, bless and praise His name.

● Pray in the Holy Spirit "tongues"

● Pray for healing in your soul, health, marriage, relationships, family, finances, government, economy

● Pray for your light to shine and for great outpourings of the Holy Spirit to be manifested

● Decree that you are healed, redeemed and released from calamities, catastrophes and any hidden dangers that would try to come up against you, health, marriage, relationships, family, finances, government, economy

Prayer

Jehovah Rapha, You are the God who heals and delivers us from all manner of disease! You are the Lord my physician. You are the Lord, my life-giver. You are the Lord who makes me immune to diseases. You are the Lord who brings only health. You are making me whole and _____ [mention in prayer anyone who needs healing]. I declare that Christ has redeemed me from the curse of the law [Galatians 3:13]. Sickness has no legal right to attack or attach itself to my body or life. Surely, he hath borne our griefs, and carried our sorrows: yet we did esteem him stricken, smitten of God, and afflicted. But he was wounded for our transgressions, he was bruised for our iniquities: the chastisement of our peace was upon him; and with his stripes we are healed [Isaiah 53:4-5]. Jesus has carried away every sickness, disease, dysfunction, disorder, and diagnosis in the name of Jesus. I refuse to accept sickness, and I will not tolerate it. I command it to go, now in Jesus' name! I decree, for this very reason was the Son of God made manifest — to destroy the works of the devil. The set hour for refreshing for God's people is NOW, it's here! I am healed, I have recovered, and I am restored holistically in the name of Jesus! Amen!

Reflect and write what the Lord is sharing with you during your time of prayer.

_____

_____

_____

_____

_____

_____

_____

_____

_____

_____

_____

_____

_____

_____

_____

_____

_____

_____

_____

_____

_____

_____

_____

_____

_____

NOTES

Watch Six (9am-Noon)

"For no matter how many promises God has made, they are 'Yes' in Christ" **2 Cor 1:20 (NIV)**

O Lord, You are the Promise Keeper and You are faithful to ALL of your promises, loving towards ALL you have made [Psalm 145:13]. During this sixth watch of prayer, I declare that Your promises are now invading my reality in the name of Jesus. I thank You that all of the promises of God are yes and amen! I thank You, Lord that during this watch, I receive by faith the supply of all resources needed for every assignment, place and calling You have assigned for me to fulfill. I lay claim that You have promised to strengthen me, give me rest, take care of all of my needs, to answer when I call, to cause everything to work out for my good, to be with me, to protect me, and You have promised me deliverance! You promised to never fail, to always be good! You are never slack concerning Your promises, so I thank You that during this watch, promises are manifesting! I vow to give You glory and honor, it all belongs to You! This is the Lord's doing, and it's marvelous in my eyes [Psalm 118:23]! I thank You for all the promises that are now activated because of Christ's sacrifice on the cross. I lay hold to life and life more abundantly because of Jesus! In Jesus' name, Amen!

Reflect and write what the Lord is sharing with you during your time of prayer.

_____

_____

_____

_____

_____

_____

_____

_____

_____

_____

_____

_____

_____

_____

_____

_____

_____

_____

_____

_____

_____

_____

NOTES

Watch Seven (Noon-3pm)

"Arise, shine, for your light has come, and the glory of the LORD rises upon you." **Isaiah 60:1 (NIV)**

Father, I invite your presence into this space as I take a moment to reverence your grace and mercy. You are my strength, my aid in trouble, and my hedge of protection. You are the God who brings rivers of running water to the desert. Father, I thank you for giving me this day. May this day bring supernatural opportunities, divine favor, and blessings from heaven. Guide my steps and allow today to yield its best fruit to me. Shed your light on all things that seem hidden. Give me clarity for all things that seem clouded. When the challenges of life arise, my faith will take root in Your Word according to Isaiah 43:19 (ESV), "I will make a way in the wilderness and rivers in the desert." I pray in alignment with Your reputation and Word, "He made streams come out of the rock and caused waters to flow down like rivers" [Psalm 78:16 (ESV)].

Give me the aptitude to pray until there is a breakthrough. Give me the strength and endurance to overcome difficult and complex situations/circumstances through prayer. Father, remove all doubt, frustration, and exhaustion from me and allow me to operate in the mercy, grace, and strength of God. In Jesus' name, Amen!

Reflect and write what the Lord is sharing with you during your time of prayer.

_____

_____

_____

_____

_____

_____

_____

_____

_____

_____

_____

_____

_____

_____

_____

_____

_____

_____

_____

_____

_____

_____

_____

_____

NOTES

Watch Eight (3pm-6pm)

"I have been crucified with Christ and I no longer live, but Christ lives in me. The life I now live in the body, I live by faith in the Son of God, who loved me and gave himself for me."
Galatians 2:20 (NIV)

Father, thank you for your love and peace that surpasses all earthly understanding. I ask that you wrap me in your love and peace today. God, You gave us the greatest sacrifice, and for that I say thank you. I am so grateful for the benefits we receive because of the death, burial, and resurrection of Jesus. Thank you for laying down your life, so we can be a part of your Kingdom. Thank you for delivering us from the grip of eternal sin and offering your love and forgiveness to us daily. I pray for a mighty deliverance upon the people of this world, that they may be set free from anything that is not the Father's Will. Please give your people the grace to walk in Resurrection Life and all its benefits. Jehovah Nissi, I ask that You wave Your banner of victory over all believers! Thank you, LORD, for being a Father and guide to all your children. I pray for the nations and all souls coming into the kingdom. I pray that the earth will be filled with the knowledge of the Lord, that all people will fear You and walk upright before You. I thank you that the people of God will turn to His marvelous light and that the blood of Jesus prevails over his people. I pray that the same righteousness and justice that is around the foundation of the Lord's throne be ever present in the Body of Christ. Enable us to be conduits of change, light, and glory! I declare that the people of God will turn away from the works of darkness into Your marvelous light. In the name of Jesus' we seal this prayer, Amen.

Reflect and write what the Lord is sharing with you during your time of prayer.

_____

_____

_____

_____

_____

_____

_____

_____

_____

_____

_____

_____

_____

_____

_____

_____

_____

_____

_____

_____

_____

_____

_____

_____

_____

_____

_____

_____

NOTES

Final Word

There is a movement of prayer taking place all over the planet that is firmly rooted in Scripture. It is the call of God to His people to take their places on the wall as watchmen. Whether we look to the Old Testament or the New, we find that God is calling us to watch and pray.

Our modern culture does not readily identify with the ancient concept of watchmen on the walls. To accept the Lord's call to this great movement of prayer then, we will need to train ourselves in what it means to be a part of this great company of the "alert." The Isaiah 62 passage, quoted above, helps us greatly in this task.

It is clear that the job of a watchman is a continual commitment. It is not sporadic or dependent upon our feelings. Because of the life or death nature and constancy of the watchman's task, it is an assignment for the many, not just the one. Believers working in tandem, sharing shifts of prayer, will be the most effective.

Isaiah 62:6-7 describes an intensity that must be shared…day and night…never silent…give yourself no rest. Only groups of committed believers who band together in watchful prayer will be able to stay at their post.

Notice also in Scripture that it is God who posts the watchmen. This is a divine assignment, not just the latest prayer fad. To stand on the wall as a watchman, stationed there by the Lord Himself, is a great privilege. We need to receive and obey such a call with gratitude and humility.

Perhaps the overwhelming characteristic of watchman prayer is that it is to be done with open eyes. This does not necessarily imply physical eyes, although it certainly can, but our spiritual eyes must be held wide open. We are to watch and pray.

What is it we are looking for as we pray? I would suggest that we first look for an enemy attack. Certainly in Old Testament times, this sort of defensive watchfulness was at the heart of the task. The watchman on the wall was always on the alert for any attempt of an enemy to attack or infiltrate the city. Too many times, the walls of the Church and of our cities today are open to attack because of a lack of watchfulness. In 2 Corinthians 2:11, Paul wrote that we are "not unaware" of the schemes of the enemy. Unless praying watchmen are on duty, we too often find ourselves painfully unaware of the attempts of the enemy to disrupt and destroy.

On the opposite end of matters, I believe that the watchmen are also to keep their eyes open to see and discern moves of God. All too often we miss out on what God is doing because we are not paying attention. The watcher should be always asking, "Lord, what are You doing in our church or city this day? Is there something You are calling Your people to do in cooperation with what You are doing?" How much more effective we would be if, instead of starting our own projects for God, we found ourselves moving alongside a current move of God! The other area for watchfulness is discerning the needs of the people of God. A watchman on the wall in the Old Testament would often see human needs and be able to send someone to meet those needs. Is there someone among you who is prayerfully watching the people of God to see who is hurting, or who is in need? We often talk about shepherding the flock of God.

What greater way to shepherd than to continually watch in prayer over the sheep the Lord loves?

What will be the results of watchmen prayers? According to Isaiah, we will see the firm establishment of the Kingdom of God. The prophet speaks of the establishment of Jerusalem, the dwelling place of God among His people. In both the Old and the New

Covenant, Jerusalem represents God among man. Jesus' main message was the coming kingdom, present in Him. Emmanuel... God with us! Another result of this powerful prayer movement will be that the glory of God will be seen among the nations. As we watch and pray, we find ourselves lining up with the prophet Habakkuk and crying out for the glory of God to cover the earth "as the waters cover the sea" (**Habakkuk 2:14**). Prayer warriors, it is time to ascend the wall of your city and begin to fulfill your calling as watchmen of God.

Take this time to reflect and write what the Lord is sharing with you after reading this prayer manual. What are you hearing the Lord say? What are your key takeaways? Write out your thoughts and prayers of your own.

_____

_____

_____

_____

_____

_____

_____

_____

_____

_____

_____

_____

_____

_____

_____

_____

_____

_____

_____

_____

_____

_____

_____

Notes

Contact C. Shaemun Webster

Contact C. Shaemun Webster on his various social media platforms:

Facebook: @pastorshaemun
Instagram: @pastorshaemun
Website: www.cswministries.com
Email: cswebsterministries@gmail.com

www.ingramcontent.com/pod-product-compliance
Lightning Source LLC
Chambersburg PA
CBHW060227030426
42335CB00014B/1361